D1159433

Photographers Credits

T. Abe, Bon Color, M. Ezaki, Y. Futagawa,
Y. Ishimoto, Kawasumi Architectural Photograph Office,
T. Kitajima, S. Mishima, O. Murai, S. Nagaoka,
K. Sekiya, Shinkenchiku-sha Co., Ltd, Shokokusha,
R. Takase, Y. Takase

Editorial Director USA
Pierantonio Giacoppo

Chief Editor of Collection
Maurizio Vitta

Publishing Coordinator
Franca Rottola

Graphic Design
Paola Polastri

Editing
Jesse Oona Nickerson

Colour-separation
Litofilms Italia, Bergamo

Printing
Poligrafiche Bolis, Bergamo

First published January 1997

ISBN 88-7838-021-0

Kiyonori Kikutake

Kiyonori Kikutake

From Tradition to Utopia

Preface by
Kiyonori Kikutake

Introduction by
Maurizio Vitta

Contents

Preface

by Kiyonori Kikutake

First of all I wish to express my fundamental architectural views, in other words, the basic items that form my philosophy and thinking models on architecture. I was born in Kyushu in 1928, the year CIAM was formed. In Kyushu, there is a vast plain call Tsukushi Plain. At the time, it was considered the most fertile agricultural land for rice production in Japan. In the middle of the best rice producing district in Japan runs the Chikugo River with its abundant water. My family had been the landlord of this plain for many generations.

In succession I happened to be the 17th generation. This area is graced with four beautiful seasons. Its climate is richly varied, summer is extremely hot with much sunlight, spring and autumn are pleasantly mild, and in winter the grounds are covered with snow. In June, which is a very wet month, rice is planted .

Water covers the entire surface of the area. When summer has passed and autumn comes there is the harvesting season. After the rice is reaped, beans, Chinese milk vetch, colza, buckwheat and other grains that are planted between the rows of rice are gathered. When this work is completed, in autumn, wheat is planted . After two to three months, it is harvested. In other words, it is a double-cropping. On the west side of this fertile plain is the Sefuri Mountain Range which shields the north wind coming from Korea. On the east is the range of Mt. Kabuto. The river flows into the Sea of Ariake and on its banks many different products grow abundantly.

There are pictures of rafts, made of fallen timber from the forests, being delivered upstream. Beneath the Sea of Ariake once there were coal mines and submarine coals used to be freely excavated. Kurume was the distributing center of rice. Kurume was also a very important agricultural distributing center. From here, rice was shipped to Osaka and Kanto.

I was raised in this place. Its seasonal sceneries and traditional

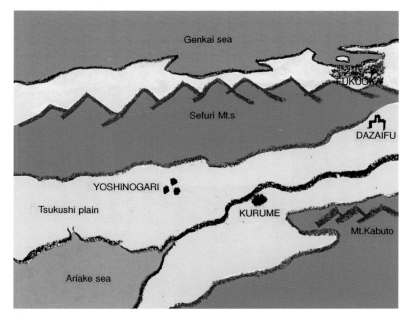

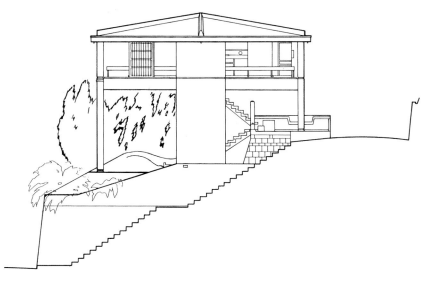

festivals are inherently suited to my fundamental views. Recently, from the land that once was mine, ruins from the 3rd and 4th century, called Yoshinogari, were discovered. Reared in this type of environment, my first job after graduation from university was rebuilding, remodeling and relocating many wooden architectures. This was my job for many years. From this, I learned that wooden architecture possesses a superb structural system: the possibility of dismantling and reassembling it. In other words, a recycling system had quite ingeniously been developed. I couldn't have learned this during my student life. My outlook on Japanese architecture, especially wood constructions, began to evolve at this point.

I began to seriously consider methods that utilize natural resources without waste, that reuse materials by dismantlement and reassembly and allow for reconstruction. One of the primary considerations on the "Metabolism Movement" was the evolution of this thought and its application to "Modern Architecture." After the first intuition I then considered situations where the application of this ingenious reconstruction can occur. Architectural space was categorized into two types: one that will eventually need reconstruction, and the other whose utilization will be permanent. That part which requires reconstruction was to be designed to actively allow dismantling, reassembling and

rebuilding. The most important part was to be placed in the core of the structure. The "Sky house" was designed around the time of this thought process. It was built in 1958. A house called "Sky house", my own residence, was where the experimentation on a house with a changeable system was carried out. It was in the "Sky house" that efforts were made to apply the foundation of my architectural philosophy. It was here that my thought process furthered to arrive at the solution of applying the concept of wooden architecture to modern architecture by using a reinforced concrete or steel frame .

With the assignment of permanent type spaces - spaces where changes are not needed - as main spaces, and spaces where

1958   **1962**   **1977**   **1985**

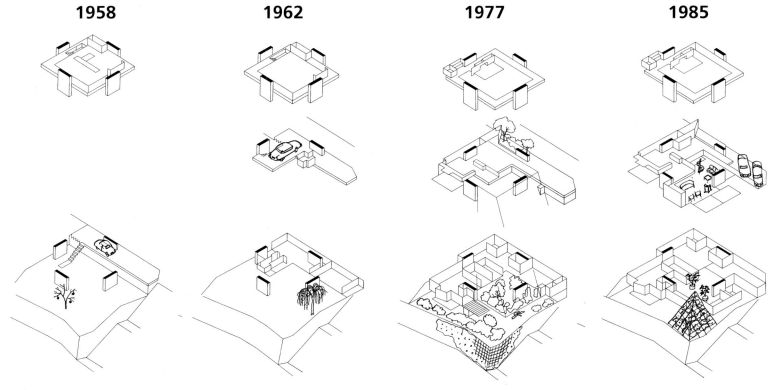

changes can be made - as subspaces with the possibility of removal- the root of the personality of this architecture begins to surface. The core of the main space of the "Sky House" is a large space reflecting the 16 tatami mat-parlour of my family house in the hometown of Kurume. (The size of rooms in a traditional Japanese house is measured in *tatamis*, or straw mats. A *tatami* is about 3 feet by 6 feet, or 18 square feet, or 0.9 metres by 1.8 metres, or 1.62 square metres.) This large parlour of 4 ken by 4 ken (1 ken is about 6 feet long) was also used in ceremonial occasions. In short, the flexibility of the house was given the utmost consideration while planning the "Sky House". A large space that can be utilized for a myriad of functions throughout the year, without restricting the lifestyle, was realized. In association with nature, many folding fixtures were used in order to control the relationship with the surrounding environment. The children's rooms, the kitchen and the bathroom were designed as units that can be moved, enlarged, decreased and changed to accommodate their predictable future needs. The uniqueness of the "Sky House" is the application of these ideas. With the "Sky House", I tried to realize spaces that can be interchanged.

With the completion of the "Sky House" in 1958, my attention was focused on extending its concept to universal application. With this in mind, I began to consider the concept of metabolism. I began thinking about it in 1958 and 1960, and once perfected, this concept was proposed at the World Design Conference.

At this point a problematical question arose: there may be complications in the realization of an architecture for mankind which is based on the idea of using a structure that can be changed like the metabolism changes. It may also be difficult to perfect everything that has already been completed and to utilize it indefinitely.

For this to occur, mechanisms that will allow changes must be contemplated and developed. As an example, there is the concept of the roof truss. When the Japanese and the Western roof trusses are compared, the latter roof truss is more practical against a short period load of instantaneous wind speed. Its dynamic strength, allows coverage of large spans with a minimal amount of materials. However, when reconstruction is required, after 30 to 40 years, Japanese roof trusses have an advantage from the point of view of reusing materials. Also from the renovation aspect, where flexibility

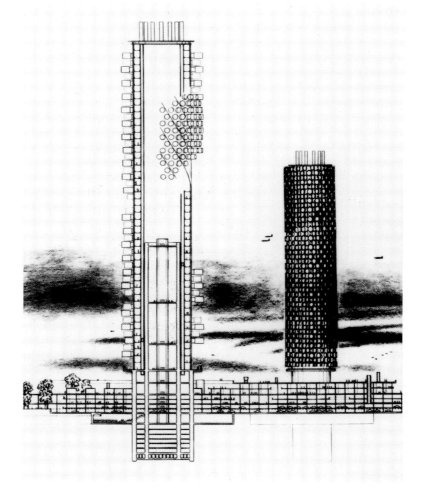

is needed for dimensional changes, because of the increase or decrease of the spans, the Japanese roof truss is more favorable.

The reasons for the ingenious development of Japanese wood joinery, especially for right angle joints and end joints, are generally attributed to the fondness of models and ornament. However, because of the possibility to develop numerous extremely imaginative end joints, they necessarily should be produced in various shapes in order to permit the removal and replacement of damaged portions, or complete pieces of roof truss members due to the extended and over time use, or to other causes. The technique employed in Japanese roof trusses holds much rationality. It clearly expresses the concept of "Metabolism".

Several projects were proposed for the realization of the concept of "Metabolism". A couple of these were the "Marine City" and the "Tower Shaped Community". If the "Marine City" were to become a typical urban space whose parts or sections can be exchanged and replaced, to allow such feats it would have to float on water .

Thus, the "Floating Marine City" was proposed. Just like the "Tower Shaped Community", in order to collectivize the residences, was composed of a basic urban structure to which residential units could to be attached.

The "Tower Shaped Community" was seriously

considered to suggest a kind of mechanism that could permit attachment. When this proposal was made, land was scarce. To counterface this condition, the walls were to be considered as vertical lands onto which residential units were to be secured.

The tower which provided the vertical lands was to be 300 meters tall. I wanted this to be the opportunity which would greatly change general thinking on the urban environment.

There still remained a large issue: methodology. I started to think about design methods when I was trying to create an architecture which would satisfy the program that was created for the design of "Cho-no-ya" (the administration building of the Izumo Shrine). However, I realized that a program is not necessarily immutable. I understood the difficulty in

designing an architecture based strictly on the program of the Shrine. What was to be done then? I remembered what in the Japanese culture represents the concept of "Ka" (the Visional Approach). I thought that "Ka" must be identified during the design process. I pondered on the issues of "Ka" (the Visional Approach) and "Katachi" (the Functional Approach).

At that time, there were three physicists in the Kyoto University, doctors Yukawa, Sakata and Taketani who proposed a theory on *meson*. Doctor Taketani proposed a methodology and from it, he determined the existence of *meson*. I received an extremely strong incentive from this theory and began to reflect deeply on it as a possible methodology. He had mentioned that in thinking, there are three stages: the stage of phenomenon, the stage of the actual condition, and the stage of substance. When considering the structure of an object, its essence can be determined through these three stages. When these stages are applied to design stages, I believe the "Katachi" step is analogous to the phenomenon stage, the actual condition stage or the technical step is the "Kata" step, and the substance stage is the vision and image or the "Ka" stage. With this reflection, the three stage methodology for my architecture was completed.

In Japanese culture "Kata" is found in the traditional disciplines of flower arrangement, judo, the tea ceremony, and others. Therefore, I have strongly affirmed the importance of the technology of the immutable "Kata".

From the point of view of the methodological process, I wondered where "Modern Architecture" can be placed in chronological history. For example, in "The Fifth Generation in Architecture", I proposed a new interpretation regarding the world's change to modern architecture in the last 150 years due to the Industrial Revolution. Furthermore, in reference to Japanese architecture, I have professed the "Theory of Evolution every 400 years" which states that changes occur every 400 years.

The present is at the intersection of these two points of view. I believe that, in one way or another, Japan has a mission to lead architecture to a new direction, and that Japan's role in the modern architectural continuum will be

great. From this methodological viewpoint, I feel that it will be necessary for its architecture to participate in the mingling of cultures. The Japanese architects who, by accomplishing this have, symbolized this goal are Isoya Yoshida, Tetsuro Yoshida and Togo Murano. I believe that there are other architects from various different countries who have attained similar results. These architects transfused into the rigid and inflexible architecture of Western Culture, the different and foreign aspects of renewability and openness of Japanese architecture and created new architectural styles. I wonder what roles Japanese or Asian architecture will shoulder, compared to the roles provided by historical European architecture, Greek architecture, or the Colonial American Style.

On top of these aspects one can add subjects such as industrialization and technologies for mega-structures and system buildings. The direction for the coming new architecture will be the importance placed in the idea that the artificial environment will be created through the repetition of much accumulated social experience, obtained from the usage of artificial materials and industrialized mechanical technologies. This idea is the theme for system buildings as well as for macro-engineering of megastructures. Subsequently, subjects such as ultra highrise buildings, floating linear cities and

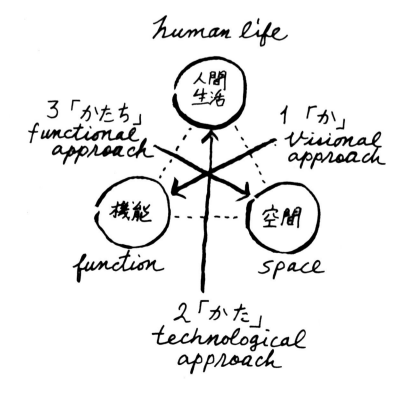

enormous domes were considered.

Considering a project with an enormous dome, I have been proposing a compression dome, contrary to those seen up to the present. Studies on these types of domes, which are made of identical members and identical joints to cover immense spaces, have been going on for a long time now. In reference to research on ultra highrise buildings, proposals to use tension wire construction on these, with a new technological application, are being made for its realization. These numerous studies are the extensions of my views on modern architecture, which is placed on top of my interpretation of accumulated technologies for traditional Japanese wooden architecture.

The above summary is my approach to architecture as well as my continuing objective.

History and Utopia

by Maurizio Vitta

Architecture's primary role in the twentieth century has been to resolve the dualism existing between imagination and function, poetry and technology, between history and utopia. The first half of the century has tried to dialectically compose the implicit conflict between these couples of concepts through the modernist ideological commitment; the second half, more than anything, has denied its possibility and given each of the terms in the couple the freedom of operating alone, confronting each other time at a time according to individual choices or emerging tendencies.

Most recent architecture has suffered from a particular kind of distress for the dissolution of the rigidly normed thought systems that have characterized the fall of "the great narrations" described by Francois Lyotard. Yet it has given its own decisive contribution to this vaster cultural phenomenon: if nothing else, it has shown how the postmodern condition has brought to the surface the primary contradiction of our time - the deep furrow dug between being and doing - not so much in the subjective perception of the world, as in its operative methods of construction. The great problems deriving from the organization of living spaces, new materials, and the social drama of big urban centers didn't appear so simple and empirically concrete expressions of theoretical concepts, but as the very substance of which our daily existence feeds on, and in which late-modern thought sees its horizon of uncertainty, bewilderment and negation. In a similar context, the dualism that has marked the development of twentieth century architecture culture assumes a decisive importance: however it cannot be reduced to a simple mirror-image of a generalized existential condition, in other words it is a reference point for an anthropological and philosophical reflection anchored to the reality of things.

The first to propose a comprehensive analysis of the dualistic terms that came to be the centre of architects' attention was the Japanese architecture world. The first response was the 1960's Metabolism theory, which wasn't an architectural theory, but a critical theory of society analyzed from the architecture perspective.

The fact that it wasn't merely an answer in solution to Japan's overpopulation problem, as appeared initially, is demonstrated by the fact that those first reflections were coherent even with the following developments of culture and society; and even if they weren't the only ones, and could give way to critics and reservations, nonetheless, in their evolution they have drawn a general portrait of the postmodern condition, in which architecture plays the role that history has assigned to it.

Japanese sensitivity in overcoming contradictions by continuously researching their point of maximum balance is in fact implicit in the history and culture of this country that has traditionally had to deal with profound contrasts and lacerations. Architecture has witnessed this very fact on its own skin: there isn't one Japanese building that doesn't repropose the theme of contradiction between temporariness and permanency, casuality and necessity, tradition and modernism. However the solution to this problem has always been found on the ground of temporal dynamics, instead of structural space: the concept of *continuity* is defended by that of *renewal,* which is its opposite; and mobile space arrangement assures the development of coded functions. Harmony between opposites is thereby not achieved inside the architectural structure - as happened from the beginning in western architecture, in its tentative to arrive at a meeting point between form and function - but outside it, in the physical and historical context in which it is claimed, making it pulsate at its own rhythm.

Among Japanese architects, Kyonori Kikutake is one of the most susceptible to this subject. He has been a protagonist of the first Metabolist period. But his architecture has not suffered from second thoughts or fluctuations:

his last works - whether just projects or actual realizations - express the same aesthetic and ethical tension of the beginning; and even if during the years his thoughts regarding design have become freer and more complex, nonetheless they still rest on the same grounds. His commitment towards living spaces is unaltered. The work with which this volume closes is the extreme end of a research that began at the time of *Marine City*.

Perhaps the constant factors in Kikutake's architecture are more significant than the innovations.

This designer's attachment to the history and culture of Japan is equal to that of other Japanese architects. In addition, however, he is deeply rooted, in a material sense, to his land and to its reality; and he transforms this element into a design criterion, or an architectural poetic. His work begins, not accidentally, in 1958 with the construction of the *Sky House,* which was at the same time his home and also the house where his architecture was born. In this building the structure digs its conceptual roots in the idea of a house as a living cell, that participates in the life of its inhabitants. Kikutake saw, in the fact that its construction elements could be renewed in time and could be placed freely in the interior to adapt to everchanging necessities, the possibility of an architecture which is not only able to shelter human existence but that

can actually be a part of it. The *Marine City* project with which, almost contemporarily, he signed a sort of Metabolist Manifesto, didn't but transfer to a collective dimension the same principles of an architecture which is able to grow in perfect syntony with the life of its inhabitants.

In his latest works, Kikutake's design philosophy has followed along this path, and on its way he has made its foundation elements ever clearer. It is present in all his works; however analytically it is possible to distinguish its main components throughout all his works, by grouping together the various proposals, only in the intention of giving a more accurate description.

After his own saying, Kikutake profoundly lives the experience of his origins. He is deeply rooted to the history of his land, not only in purely intellectual terms, but, one could say, with an intense physical bond to the land in which he was born.This rooted attachment expresses itself in his architecture, in the crushed forms of many of his buildings, that stick to the floor as if in an embrace. The *Oita Marine Culture Center* is the best example of this: the construction distends along the ground, almost touching it with its extremity; and its tenderly curved outline visually expresses the intimate relationship between sea and land that is formed by the nucleus of the Japanese islands.

However, notwithstanding this bond, there is no desire of mimesis. His architecture doesn't try to camouflage itself with the landscape nor to copy its configuration. It remains to the end what it is, i.e. an artifact. In fact the attachment to the environment is really born from the respect of reciprocal identities: architecture and nature penetrate one within the other, without blending. The act of embracing the earth is in large amount symbolic. It is, in a way, a conceptual gesture; and it is architecture's sign of expressiveness - the great arch that covers the path like an uncertain boundary between human artifice and natural spontaneousness - to reveal its abstract reality.

The dome structure present in many of Kikutake's last projects eloquently confirms this tendency. In western culture domes more than anything have a transcendent meaning: extreme examples are the Pantheon, of the Roman era, and Michelangelo's dome for St. Peters'. However, the criterion of transcendence imposes that of emergency, detachment from the world's physical reality, upward tension; and although contemporary architecture has almost cancelled its symbolic value in the name of purely functional needs, making it become the ideal roofing for big collective spaces, the dome still remains an irreplaceable *tòpos* in western architecture culture.

Kikutake has resumed the contemporary theme of the dome intended as a structural element for the social rituals of our time - sports, entertainment, meetings - but here also he worked on the concept of rooted attachment to the earth which is present in his other works: the *Nijigata Theater Complex, the Kumamoto Prefecture Public Sports Arena,* the *Toyama Prefecture Multi-Purpose Arena,* the *Media Dome of Kita-Kyushu,* are all projects that insist on a linked relationship between architecture and soil. The *Art Museum* that will rise on the banks of the Shinjiko lake also confirms the same attraction to the ground, although it doesn't have a dome roof.

Obviously there is a concern of not weighing on the landscape - whether urban or natural - with structures that will inevitably greatly affect its features. A flat building reduces the architectural visual impact and diminishes the pain of cities and nature, which are too often raped by eccessive intervention. However, it is possible to read more profound meanings in the image of a big roof distending over the earth in an act of what appears to be, at the same time, devotion and protection. In this attachment to the earth, the dome finds again the transcendence, that in Western culture had been looked for by pushing up towards the sky; and even if it is a secular transcendence, which feeds on social relations and urban culture, nonetheless it

expresses values that belong to the sphere of collective ethics.

Such values are revived in different ways in others of Kikutake's works. The profound concept of attachment to his land reminds us of certain relations to tradition, to which late-modern thought has returned to reflect upon deeply, as is well known. A small architectural jewel such as the *Jizaitei,* a space destined to conversation and mutual consideration, explicitly illustrates the typically Japanese anxiety of attributing a strongly rooted identity to continuity of customs and traditions. However the issue has not been faced and resolved only on a formal basis or, if preferable, in linguistic terms. This work unveils a more profound research. In it architecture confronts itself not only with space but with time : it isn't satisfied with the transformation of geometric space into historical space, in other words, a replacement of memory, it heads towards a superior form of balance, a temporal dimension rendered fixed and unchangeable by architectural dimension. In a certain way, it could be said that in this small construction the arcitectural structure lives as a temporal structure, i.e. as present vitally rooted into the past. Japanese culture has been careful in the last half century to assure continuity, not by means of simple reproduction of the forms of the past, but by seizing it through allusions and signals in the corpus of an architecture that is inspired by the principles of modernism. But Kikutake has always been particularly sensitive in combining in the body of the construction the essence of western modernism's geometric rigour with a formal language that is able to draw a thick network of referencess to the architectural vocabulary of the past, and hints of the complex symbolism of the Japanese cultural universe. The *Edo Tokyo Museum* represents a well known example of this consciousness. It can also be appreciated in the *Hotel Sofitel Tokyo,* due to its outline that recalls the characteristic jutting cornices of ancient Japanese constructions; or else, with a different form in the *Hanno Kusunoki Country Club,* where continuity with the past is less explicit, but not less perceptible.

The decision to underline the link with the past more or less strongly, is tied to the needs of each single project. A building like the *Kurume City Hall,* that boldly imposes itself on the urban landscape in which Kikutake himself was born, follows different criteria. Here the author seems to fully stick to the principles of twentieth century rationalism: the extremely geometric volumes, the linear and dry design, and especially the construction's marked verticality leave no doubts as to the cultural matrix of this work. However, even this case is not so much an adaptation to a style, as an interpretation in a regional key of its forming elements.

In the image of Kikutake's last architecture works, in transparency, there are the same themes that he has been pondering on since the beginning of his career. It isn't that there hasn't been an evolution in his design method: one only has to look at the technical details in his constructions, and especially his relationship to technology, to realize how far he has gone in perfecting his professional tools. However in this development, the way of thinking that makes of him an architect is still coming to grips with the same initial problems and interrogatives. As we say that great writers write the same book to the end, so Kikutake confronts himself each time, and in each project with the subjects that have fascinated and tormented him since the beginning. To be sure, in this he is vividly participating to the anguish felt by two - or three - generations of Japanese architects since the second half of the twentieth century. But as with all the others: his individuality can be reduced only within certain limits to the models of the professional culture of his time. Beyond these limits his originality is indisputable and his work must be judged within this originality.

There is no doubt that the theme proposed by Kikutake's architecture fully expresses itself as a reflection on the very dualism, that marked all the architecture culture of the twentieth century. The brief considerations on his last works amply bear witness to this argument. The interesting part is not so much in finding a generalized problematic, as in establishing the designer's solutions in answer to it.

The first topic to be handled is the relationship between tradition and modernism, by which the whole late-modern debate has been influenced. This precedence can naturally be commented: in Europe it has been strongly professed with mainly aesthetic motivations, and in Japan in the name of needs that were mostly ethical; whereas in reality it reflects on other more substantial and profound questions. Kikutake is naturally interested in this problem. However he situates it in a perspective of greater profoundness.What we called "rooted attachment to the earth" in his works isn't only a simple tension towards cultural identity or a desire to preserve a continuity with the past. In his architecture you don't find nostalgia, nor a proud rivendication of history - traps in which many late-modern projects have fallen.

His interest goes beyond all this: in a certain sense, rather anthropologically than ethnologically; it's imbued with human values, not regional idols.

In fact, in Kikutake's work the

element that instead characterizes most late-modern western architecture is lacking: i.e. the regionalist *pathos.* Obscure to him are the stressing of historical primary forms, the obsessive insistence on traditional materials, the emphasis on styles of the past, the accumulation of classical elements that one notices in many European or American buildings. Whereas in his projects one can see a certain reserve that induces him to proceed by hints and allusions, as is common to many of his Japanese colleagues as well; or else - and this is a peculiar trait of his - to reelaborate traditional forms so that he can pull them in and make them appear in structures that are strongly bound to the present, or perhaps already projected into the future.

This design model helps reflect on the scarcity of a "regionalism" that is often invoked in end-of-the-century architecture as a cultural ground from which one can draw to exit from the drought of rationalism. Surely the revendication of local identities is a value which has been too long neglected, with known negative consequences. But clearly this kind of concept cannot imply as its main and definite result a "culture of differences": the diversity in an architectural approach is only the preface to an idea of anthropological unity on which the culture of the third millenium should found itself.

The attraction to the earth - and the rooted attachment to it as expression of continuity and modernism is one of the poles on which Kikutake's architecture sits. The other pole is technology.

In Japan, the technical problematic is experienced, as is known, on two parallel levels: on one side its instrumental, and purely utilitarian character, is glorified; on the other it is the scenario for the culture of the near future. Global computerization has already spread to the construction and management of buildings; but it is present also as a developing facility, as a cultural form to which the world must tend to in its evolution. A computerized society is, in this perspective, a society that assigns to information its physical well-being and its thought.

In Kikutake's architecture, however, the most advanced stages of contemporary technology assume a special character. In some way they are subordinated to the anthropological tension that pervades each work, becoming a tool that can realize that intimate compenetration of architecture and life, which is its main intent.

Kikutake starts out from the concept of continuous renewal of antique wooden structures, assigning these the possibility to realize structures that blend perfectly with the life of the people that inhabit them, and follow their vital rhythm. He seeks flexibility - one of the most original and complex concepts in Japanese

culture - as an objective that cannot be renounced in his architecture; however, as he knows well, it is reachable by means of a technique which is capable of making use of the most secret resources and laws of building materials.

Therefore even computer technology, in his eyes, is an anthropological element. It should be used to calculate and realize his domes that are pressed against the earth, and to assure them a following not due to the longlasting materials, but to their continuous renovation. Building, taking apart and reassembling are the typical movements in Kikutake's architecture. It doesn't matter whether they follow old mechanical formulas or if they use the new resources of cybernetics. What matters is that a building should live as a container of life. In this way architecture becomes a body holding human bodies, a vital complex pulsating in unison with human life. Computer technologies transform architectural ideas into biological concepts: from wood to new materials, controled by electronic impulses the leap is only a historical gap; continuity is assigned to the physiological function of the structure, which is destined to renew itself like an organism that incessantly regenerates.

Obviously this kind of design model calls in question the problem of architectural "form".

However, one must understand that Western culture has separated "form" from "function" a long time ago, and has now spent the last hundred years in the tentative of reuniting them once again. Japanese culture has never reached such a drastic separation, since it is founded more on synthesis than on distinction. Modernism has nonetheless put the question in different terms; and a cosmopolitan architecture cannot try to ignore this fact.

This has strongly emerged from the most recent reflections of principle Japanese architects. Kikutake himself, referring to nuclear physics, speaks, in relation to his design philosophy, of three approaches - the functional step or *katachi*, the technical step or *kata* and the poetic step or *ka*. The distinction, as often happens in these cases is convenient: whereas in reality the design process inglobes all three of them simultaneously. The problem, however, originates due to the fact that this simultaneousness doesn't give space to their reciprocal relations.

Western aesthetics has accepted to place architecture in the sphere of art, but only due to its formal qualities. The concept of "function", which is a constituent part of it, has remained marginal in philosophical consideration, almost as if it were a dishonourable aspect of its cultural individuality.

Basically the problem has remained unresolved; and in fact, it hasn't been fully solved in Japanese architecture culture either. Nevertheless, in reality, it disappears: our perception of a contemporary building spontaneously brings these three approaches to a unity.

Kikutake's insistence on architecture as "poetry" is quite meaningful at this point. First of all it assumes that a separate concept of "form" has been overcome; and then it consents to place the question of "function" in a more significant light. Speaking of "poetry" implies being open not to appearence but to meaning; or, if one prefers, to make the meaning clear and perceptible. However architecture's function almost entirely identifies itself with "function": it justifies itself in how the space that it organizes is used. At this point its functional aspects must be established. Jan Mukarovsky has shown very clearly that functionalism in architecture is a very complex phenomenon.

He individualized a "quadruple functional front" (current use, historical use, collective organization, and symbolic function); but he immediately specified that the four functions don't coincide and aren't necessarily parallel.

The concept of "poetry" formulated by Kikutake assigns a strong preeminence to the symbolic function in architecture. It will necessarily be an aesthetic concept, mainly based on perception and emotional experience - the only things that can go beyond the distinctions of analytical thought, and can give architecture back its integrity.

And however, only through this privileged channel can the strong ethical force of Kikutake's architecture emerge in its just dimension. It's as if all the other elements of his works - the technological structure, the functional destination, and the cultural origin - would converge in the sole goal of making architecture dense with poetic meaning so that its most important message - the great address to humanity and its rooted attachment to the earth - can be intended in its deepest sense. It's not by accident that Kikutake should indicate in the step of *ka* a "visionary approach".

This takes us to what can be considered the innermost nucleus of Kikutake's philosophy of the project: i.e. the relationship between history and utopia. These two terms also form a couple that the twentieth century has in vane tried to compose, whose contrast lies in the future developments of our society. In Kikutake's architecture it is a constant interrogative, formulated at the time of *Marine City* and reproposed, more or less in the same terms, in *Ecopolis*, (which is the last project in this book). Clearly, the problem of living facilities remains central. But combined with it is that of the environment, that architecture has involuntarily damaged, and is now called on to preserve and better.

The structures of *Ecopolis* almost summarize all of Kikutake's architecture conception. They originate from the lucid and rational thought of the social modernist ideology, but propose an ideal of beauty which feeds on the moral principles withheld in each large undertaking directed towards the good of human beings. Expressed in it we find an attraction towards tradition, the use of technology as an instrument of spiritual elevation, the importance of the ethic and aesthetic function. Even the attachment to the earth, which could appear contradicted by the upward skyscrapers remains quite evident in the background: the constructions take off from the ground not to detach themselves from it but to absorb its vitality.

However the value of this project goes even beyond. It covers the role of utopia as motor of civilization; and it achieves this not by denying history, as has often happened, but by trying to start from the immediate reality. With *Ecopolis* there is a concrete problem, to which this proposal offers not an abstract solution, but to the contrary, an immediately practical one. Its utopic character therefore doesn't spring from its impracticability - or from the possibility of being realized in an inestimable future. To become a concrete act it only requires a collective decision: it is utopia because it acts upon will, not on possibility; because it is placed in history - to be lived, or already experienced - and not outside it.

Only in this context is it possible to understand when Kikutake uses the word "vision" to explain his work. It is such a simple concept that it could seem complex, and it consists in placing itself in a timeflow in which the anticipation of the future is also a continuous reconsideration of the past. It is the only balanced position - fluid and dynamic - that can unite the dualism between history and utopia; and in itself it is so elusive that nobody can be sure to realize today or tomorrow a project like *Ecopolis*. But at the same time one could say that *Ecopolis* or *Marine City* belong neither to the past nor to the future. They are present in all of Kikutake' work: i.e. they are its center of inspiration, the inexhaustible reserve of project energy, from which he delves time after time, in different situations, to assure a coherent continuity of thought.

On this level architecture carries out its noblest function. Tenaciously pursuing the delicate balance between ethics and aesthetics, Kikutake glorifies its social role. He reminds not by chance that he was born on the year that CIAM was given life to, i.e. one of the greatest enterprises that architects have ever undertaken. Much of that strongly moral spirit is still present in Kikutake's personality and works. However, once again he feeds on history to project himself into the future: his philosophy, just like his architecture is the outcome of assembling, taking apart and reassembling, so that it will aways be considerate of the reality and up-to-dateness of things and will always know how to find the adequate solutions to people's needs.

Works

Teahouse Jizai-Tei
1992

The function of a *Chashitsu* (or tea room) is to create a space where a person can honour and converse thoroughly with another. Every modern man desires such a space and such an intercourse. However, such a space for such an opportunity has been gradually disappearing in modern architecture. Looking around, one realizes that, even in cities, such places are rare.

There are places everywhere to hold business talks and to have business meetings, but when it comes to having dialogues, finding a space for it is quite difficult. It could be said that this causes people to hold abjection and impoverishment in their heart.

As a nodal point to reveal anew the relationships of people to people, people to art and of people to environment, the tea room must be revived. The history of Japan indisputably shows its necessity.

It is a fact, with their pristineness and simplicity, tea rooms have had much influence in forming our wonderful culture. If one desires to make this type of a tea room today, it can be made anywhere, immediately. It can be placed in the yard, in the atrium of office buildings, in a nook of a conference room, or a lobby or in libraries, schools, hospitals, hotels, fairs and other public spaces. Modern tea rooms are culture's condensed and compacted information capsules. In these tea rooms, people sit in chairs.

(In a *Chashitsu* people sit on the floor with a definite and traditional posture.)

There should be no resistence in utilizing them by the younger generations and by the people from other countries. To sit in this room with company and have a pleasant conversation while listening to music and admiring the flower display arrangements, the scrolls and paintings in the *tokonoma* (an alcove for such purposes) would be an ultimate pleasure. If the landscape scenery were added to this, the enjoyment would be amplified. From the point of view of freedom of mind, I have named the modern tea room *Jizaitei*.

It also has this name because man's freedom is the extension of the spirit of modern culture.

A detail of the window attachment to the wooden structure and, below, a scheme of the construction. Below, an external image of the building.

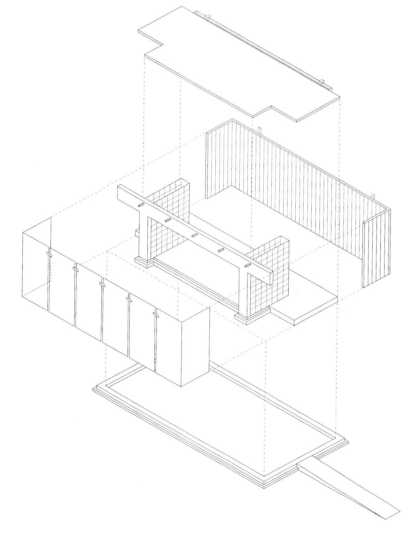

Two images of the
interior. Below,
the access ramp
and the entrance
to the building.

Oita Marine Culture Center 1992

The Bungo Strait across which the Kyushu and Shikoku islands face each other and where the Seto Inland Sea ends, is the northern limit for the tropical fish migration. In a beautiful bay area here, in the Oita Prefecture, is planned a "marine culture center" to be completed in 1992. This design makes one wonder if it derives from a fish motif, or an eye seeing a vision of the future.

One so wonders at the appearance of the center, i.e. one solid single building to endure the climatic rigor of the seaside, to shelter all necessary facilities including machinery packed in its great roof structure.

The place is a great seaside resort complex comprising a marine museum, an assembly hall, a conference hall, laboratories, restaurants, boarding accommodation, a gymnasium, etc. Visitors will fully enjoy the views of the grand sea from the building's gateway, from each floor and each room. Outdoor facilities include a swimming pool stretching 100 meters, another irregularly shaped pool for children, and a fish farm. These will be complete with outdoor restaurants, restrooms, lockers, etc. and will prepare an all-season resort. In an adjoining land piece to the east is an athletic field. Beyond it are a fishing port and a township.

This new facility will mix naturally with the local community. Because the bay area is of a convenient scale, the prefecture plans to use the environment comprehensively, as with a tree-lined path for joggers, a camp ground on an east hillside, a cycling road and a sightseeing platform. On the seashore at the foot of the hillside is a sanctuary for sea turtles; it is protected for them to lay eggs.

The maritime building is conceived also as a place for international conferences and other events but, basically, it is intended to be the "prototype" for new quiet seaside resorts where people do not rush in and out but rather settle for a while for sheer leisure time.

It is part of the Oita Prefecture's "marinopolis" concept to redevelop its southern district.

Other facilities are also under construction. And in progress in a northern part are fish farming experiments. All combined, these activities will become a new base to support offshore fishery.

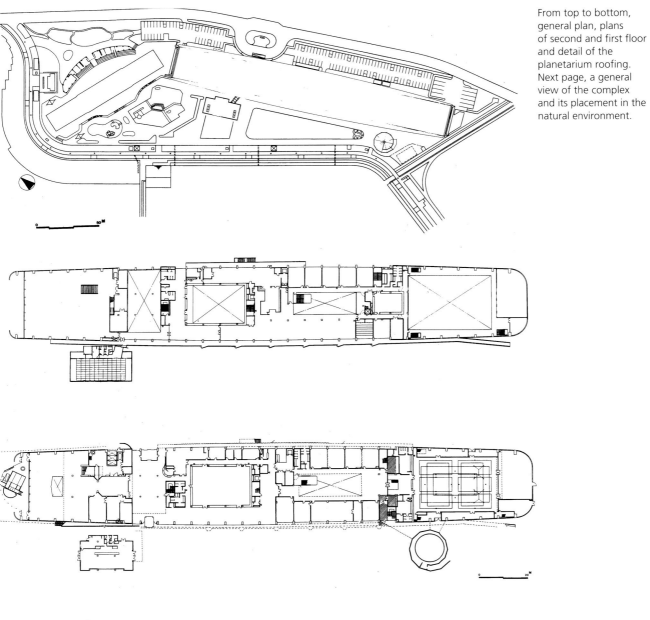

From top to bottom, general plan, plans of second and first floor and detail of the planetarium roofing. Next page, a general view of the complex and its placement in the natural environment.

This page and next page, three images of the interior spaces: atrium, entrance hall and multi-purpose room.

Niigata Theater Complex 1993

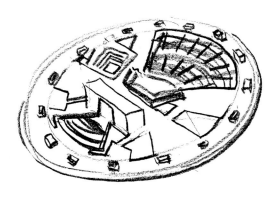

With her port facing the Sea of Japan, the city of Niigata flourished as a merchant shipping base until the Edo era. The theater complex was planned and placed for competition as an addition to the existing City Hall, the Prefecture Civic Center and the Gymnasium, all standing in the vicinity of the city park.

The facility space is protected from rain and snow. Furthermore, the proposed facility has a simple exterior appearance with a three-storey parking structure for 400 cars placed on the exterior periphery which is also used to support the snow white dome. Inside the transport dome, is a music hall which gives a feeling of openness: i.e. it is not a traditional theater that blocks outs the natural light, but theater, rehearsal room, workshop and others are all wrapped by a soft natural light and are all enveloped by the dome. The passage between these various facilities is named "Theater Lane".

This is a performance space just like a theatrical gallery, here events occurring in the theaters are introduced during the intermissions or between the shows.

It is also open as a chamber for the preservation of ceremonial attires. Furthermore, during the beginning of a performance, it becomes a private corridor only for the performers. The whole complex is achieved by placing a rooftop garden, an observation restaurant and theater shops along the exterior perimeter of the topmost floor, and by netting its circular cityscape with the Theater Lane. The unity of this facility is performing anew.

A few sketches of the
project, and a view of
the model.

ドームは外からは
白一色、夜はりで光見える

'93/2/5

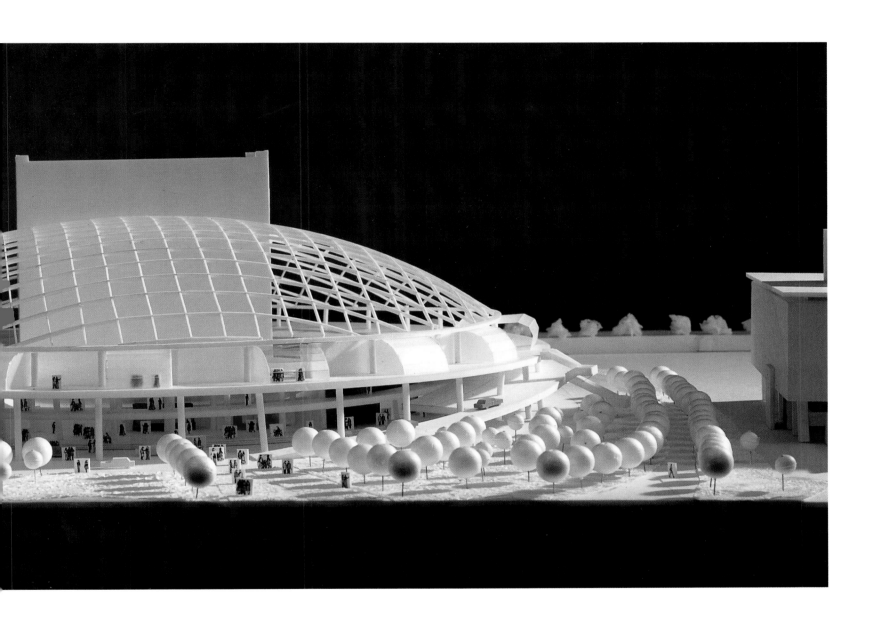

This page and next page, perspective sketch and sketch with image of interior. Below, another general view of the model.

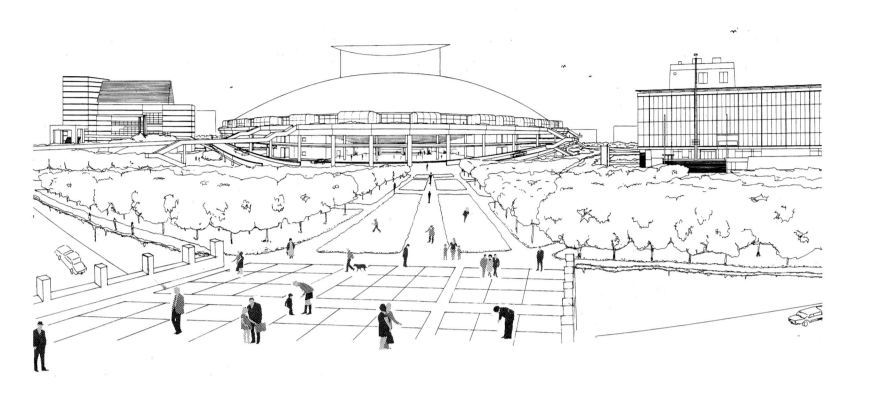

Edo -Tokyo Museum
1993

The Edo -Tokyo Museum is designed to be an urban museum that will both serve as a depository for the culture of Tokyo, or Edo as it was known until 1868, and act as a place for the creation of a new urban culture. At the same time, it will provide place where people can enjoy themselves by learning through direct experience. Located in downtown Tokyo, the building itself is characterized by its translation of the traditional forms of Japanese architecture into a modern urban museum.

Many different event spaces have been incorporated into the design, from spacious rooms for the museum's main permanent exhibits, to a vast plaza on the third floor, to the open atrium.

Space is devided functionally, with the upper portion of the building being used for the major permanent exhibits and the storage for collections, while the temporary exhibit spaces, the auditorium and the administrative offices are situated in the lower portion. Sandwiched in between these is the Edo-Tokyo Plaza. These spaces are created by means of two structural units, a superstructure and a substructure, which are supported by four massive pillars.

This arrangement makes possible a very spacious building which is flexible enough to be modified to suit future needs. The design also incorporated devices to dampen vibration and it should be little affected by earthquakes.

The permanent exhibits include both original material and copies, and they are designed to be enjoyable and easy to understand.

The exhibits illuminate the history of Edo-Tokyo, the day-to-day lives of its people and the city's arts. The museum will also be the site of many and varied cultural activities. There will be temporary exhibitions, the auditorium will be used for public lectures and events, while there are also to be rooms which can be used for educational programming.

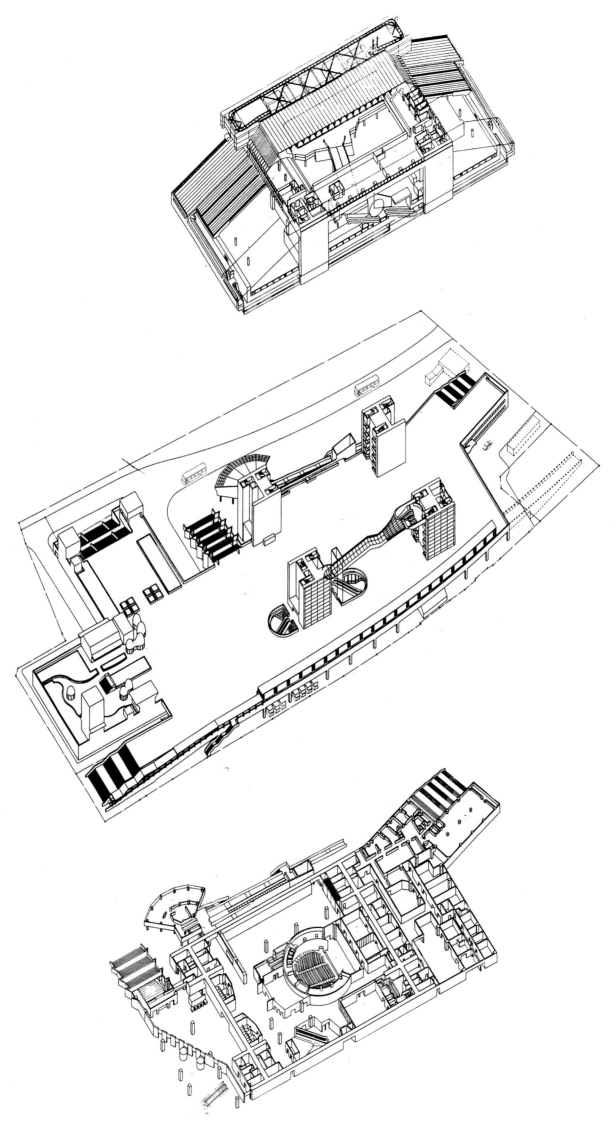

Three axonometric
views with the
functional distribution
of spaces: from top to
bottom, exhibition
level, plaza level and
hall level. Next page,
two lateral views of the
complex.

Main escalator
accessing to the upper
floors and, and next
page, detail of the
facade.

Plans of fifth, third and
first floors.

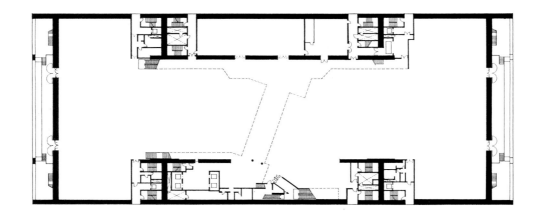

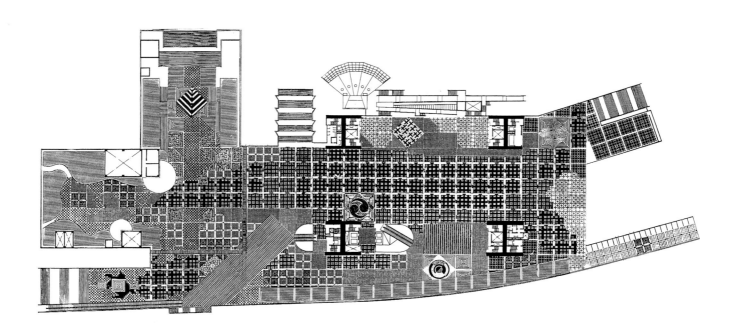

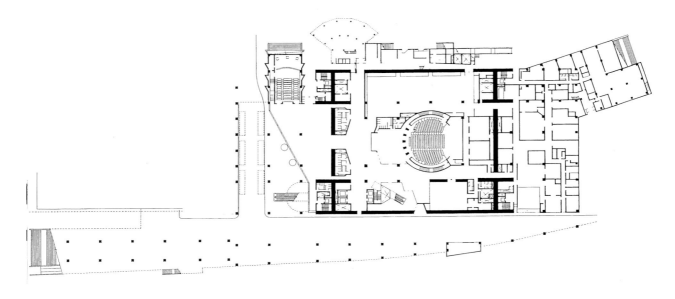

A view of rest space and, below, a view of the exhibition room.

Kurume City Hall
1994

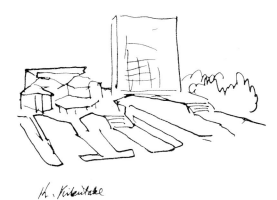

The City of Kurume is the birthplace of Kiyonori Kikutake.

It is a city located in the center of the Tsukushi Plain which represents Japan for its large and fertile agricultural region. With a population of 250,000, it is a model rural city which is shedding its old image to become the center of the new "Technopolis". The initial proposal for the City Hall Competition was an image of a high-rise city hall from where one can behold the surrounding Tsukushi Plain.

The City Hall was divided in three parts. On the lower floors are collected and placed spaces in which heavy interactions with the citizens occur. The municipal assembly is located on the top floor. Between these are located the administrative offices. The space for the administrative offices has no columns and permits sunlight through both sides as well as natural draft and ventilation.

It is an office architecture that requires only minimal energy. The City Hall and the Civic Hall, which was planned 27 years ago and completed in 1969 (see opposite image, right bottom)on the adjoining land, are harmoniously integrated to appear as one.

At the time when the Civic Center was being planned, the City Hall, with its entrance on the west side, was proposed as a future addition of the project. When the City Hall was constructed 27 years later, the location of the entrance had been changed to the south side. This was the result of a research that stated that by having a balcony on the south facade and a glass facade to the north, the building would utilize minimal energy.

The uniqueness of this City Hall is that potentially, even during a flood, the middle floor has an electrical and mechanical room that can act as a regional disaster prevention base. Furthermore, especially due to art director - Ikko Tanaka's - unwavering cooperation, traditional technical arts are constructively included in the architecture together with rich color coordinations. This original approach will certainly be given special acknowledgment.
In addition, a Japanese modern art critic - Michiaki Kawakita - also a native of Kyoto, participated in this project. It was he who suggested the method of "Arts that are Managed" : i.e. the introducing the citizens with numerous artwork by changing the displays accordingly to the situation that has been created. This will breed a pleasant atmosphere throughout the City Hall.

The building looms
with its strong image
on the urban landscape.
The section below
indicates the vertical
functional organization.
Next page, front facade.

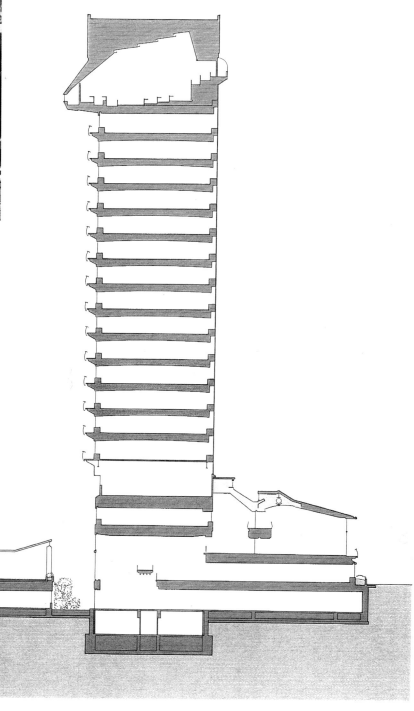

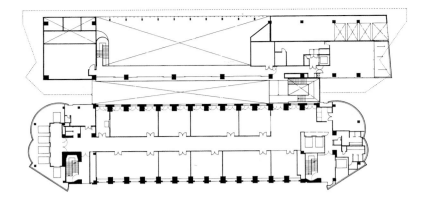

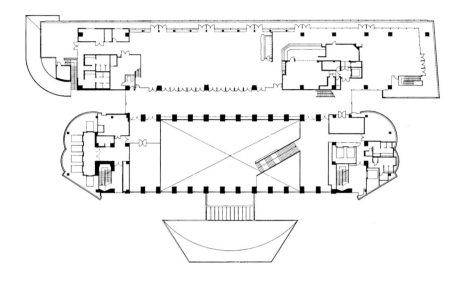

Plans of third, second and first floors,

A view of the access from the western side, and of the conference hall.

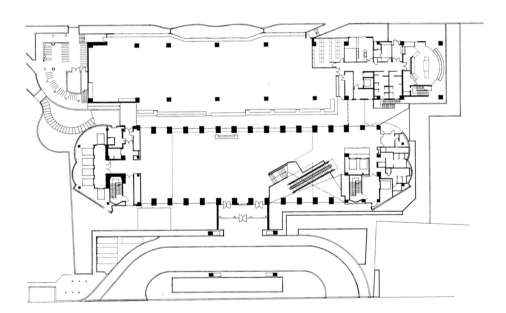

This page, upper view of entrance hall and view of multi-purpose hall. Following page, an image of the internal space.

Kumamoto Prefecture Public Sports Plaza 1994

This competition project to be built in the Kumamoto Prefecture Public All Athletic Event Park is for the creation of a sports facility where any citizen of the prefecture can casually and safely enjoy sports, recreation, cultural and other events.

As an image this shape is reminiscent of the helmet (*kabuto*) of Japanese armour. The helmet is made out of two essences, one is "*tenchu*" (the heavenly universe) and another is "*hitatare*" (an ancient court dress). "*Tenchu*" is utilized as the dome and "*hitatare*" as the arcade. The dome with its main frame of wooden lattice- work, with a grid pattern, is composed of the world's newest and the ultimate framing technology.

On top of this frame is placed a teflon membrane with a transparency rating of 25%.

With the diffusion of natural light throughout the interior, its daytime atmosphere is warm and bright, like the outdoors. During the night, like a "*chochin*" (Japanese paper lantern), the interior light penetrating through the membrane makes its silhouette look as if it were gently floating. This scene will eventually become a familiar one.

The stand, having a "U" shape, has an opening portion to permit the it to be utilized for various events. The stand's top portion has secured shades with an awning and has a good acoustic.

The "*hitatare*" arcade is a dry space area when raining and shady when bright. It offers an enjoyable and inviting space for people.

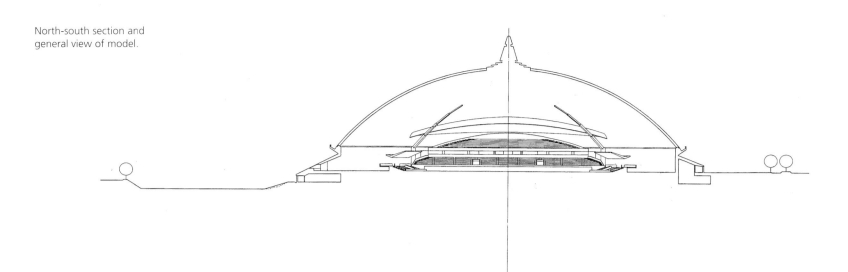

North-south section and
general view of model.

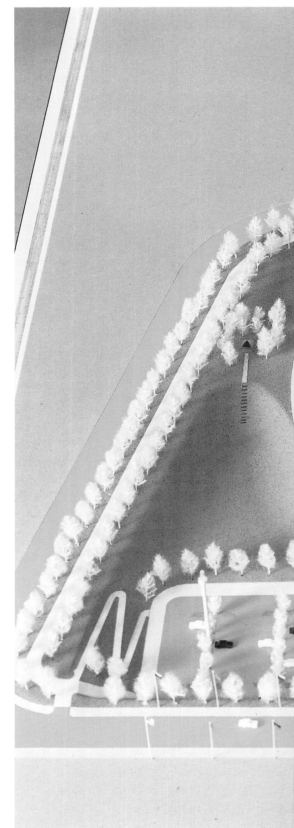

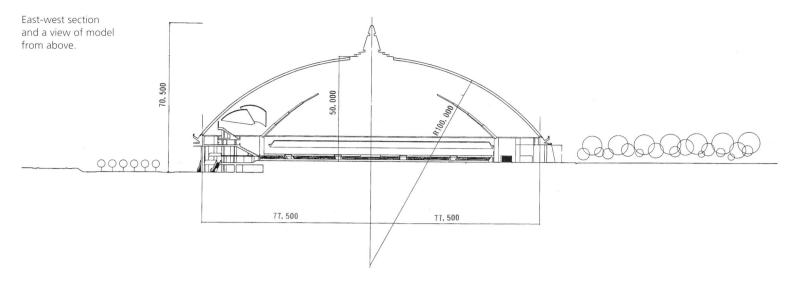

East-west section
and a view of model
from above.

70.500

50.000

R100.000

77.500   77.500

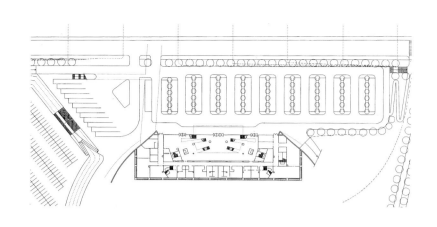

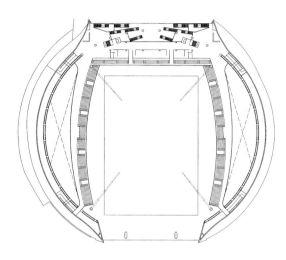

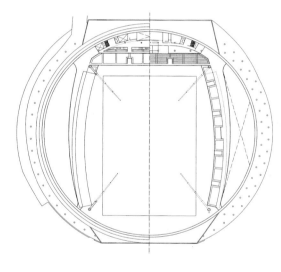

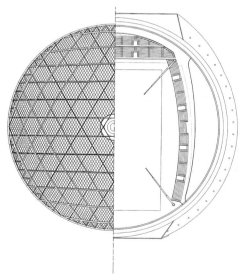

A model of the dome lit from the inside and, next page, plans of first, second, third, fourth, fifth floors and plan of roof.

The wood-made compression dome employed for Silk Road Exposition, Nara, 1988.

Hotel Sofitel Tokyo
1994

This architecture is like a lonely tree. Though it stands aloft and alone in its surrounding skyline environment, within the urban makeup, it is in harmony with the neighbouring environment, just like a giant tree serves many purposes in the forest. The approach to the project plan is based on the same concept. For example, the tower, with part of its core occupied by the elevator and utility shafts, is related to the trunk of a tree. The guestrooms are like the branches which are directly tied to the core without using the corridor. These guestrooms face the Ueno Park to the east and the Tokyo University Campus to the west, both areas have much vegetation. While they all have a view of the panorama", the 71 guestrooms made up of suites, double and twin rooms, have seven variations.

The variations in the guestrooms are expressed due to recurring set back volumes every four floors. Four floors also form a unit for the service systems. Since its silhouette resembles the "five floor pagoda", there may be people who could associate its image to the "five floor pagoda" which once stood in Ueno. The Hotel Sofitel is an extreme project which has cleared the severe regulations for the floor area ratio, the wind tunnel test and the daylight requirements.

The uniqueness of this architecture does not only appear in its upper spaces.

The ideas for lower and underground floors also share a uniqueness. In a thirty metre cube space are compactly arranged the layout of a banquet hall, a wedding hall and parking spaces .

To prevent swaying in the upper spaces of the tower, the basement is reinforced by an earth anchor.

The elevated water tank at the top, which utilizes a turned liquid column damper, has been managed because of this new technology.

Plans of second and
first floors.

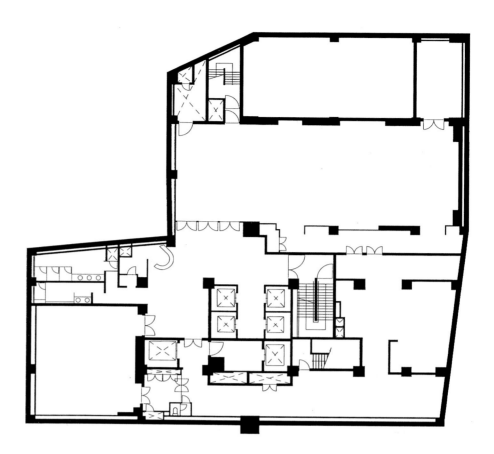

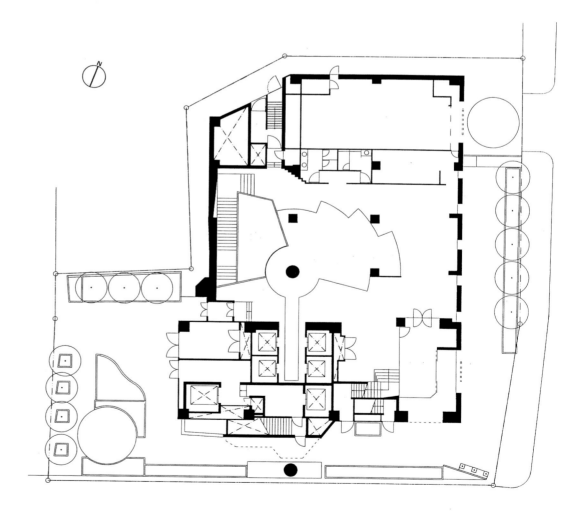

An external view of the
building and, below,
a section.

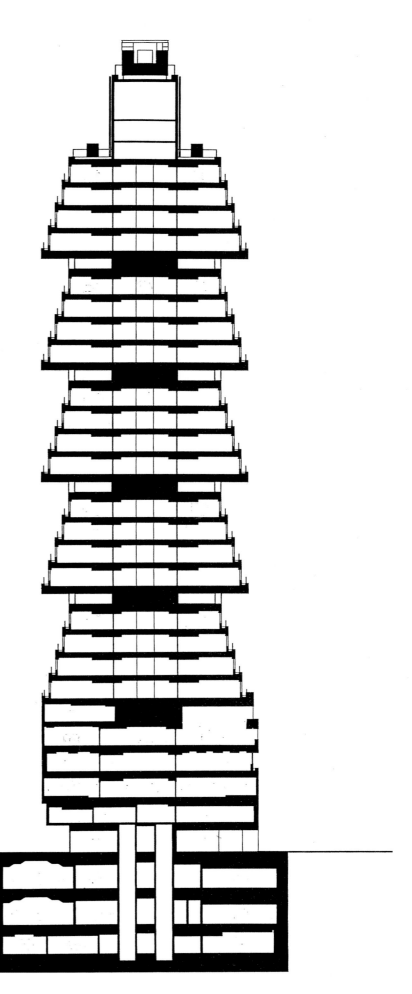

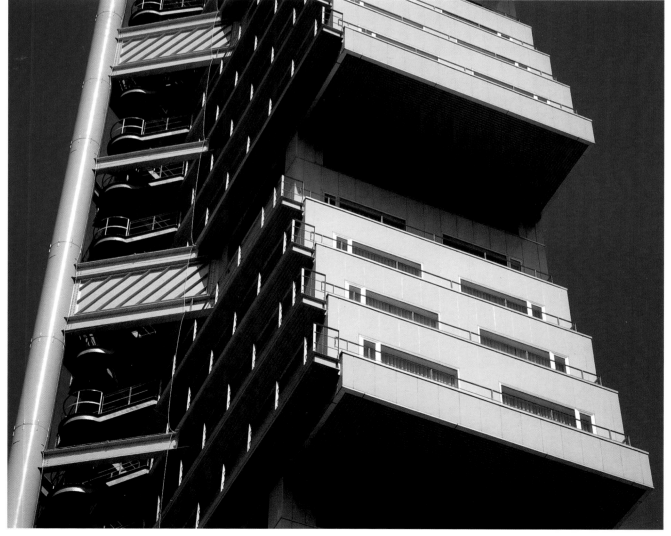

This page and next page, three details of the building's complex architecture.

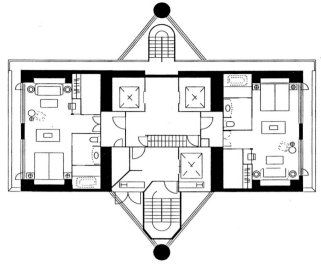

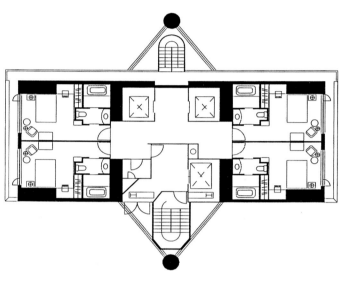

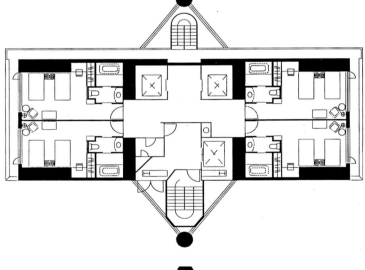

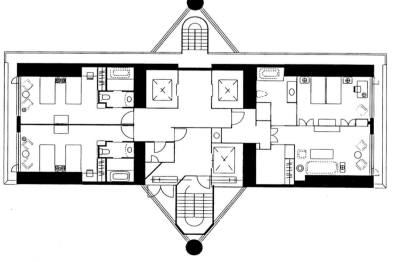

Plans of twentythird
and twentysixth floors.

Two internl views
of the building:
banquet room and
entrance hall.

Hanno Kusunoki
Country Club
1994

This country club stands on the intricate and rugged mountain range in the outskirts of Tokyo.

The clubhouse has been wedged into a small space left over between in-course and out-course. Due to this, the approach from the outside is through a tunnel that seems to barely lead visitors to the entrance.

The image of the clubhouse is that of a raised floor that has parking on the lower level and dining and locker spaces on the upper level.

The new proposed procedure prior to the start of the game is for each player, after having arrived in his car, to personally receive a cart, put his bag in it, reserve his playing time with the caddie master and park the car. Then, change clothes in the locker room and wait in the lounge from where beautiful scenery can be enjoyed. The basic idea of this procedure is for each player to do everything personally.

A good country club is said to create a warm and family-like atmosphere, due to the relationship based on mutual trust and equality between the caddies, all of the club staff and the golfers.

The objective of the project has been to create such a country club.

It is hoped that this country club will stimulate the growth of good country clubs, i.e. those which have discarded commercialism and a nouveau riche image.

General plan of area,
with position
of buildings and a detail
of the architectural
structures.

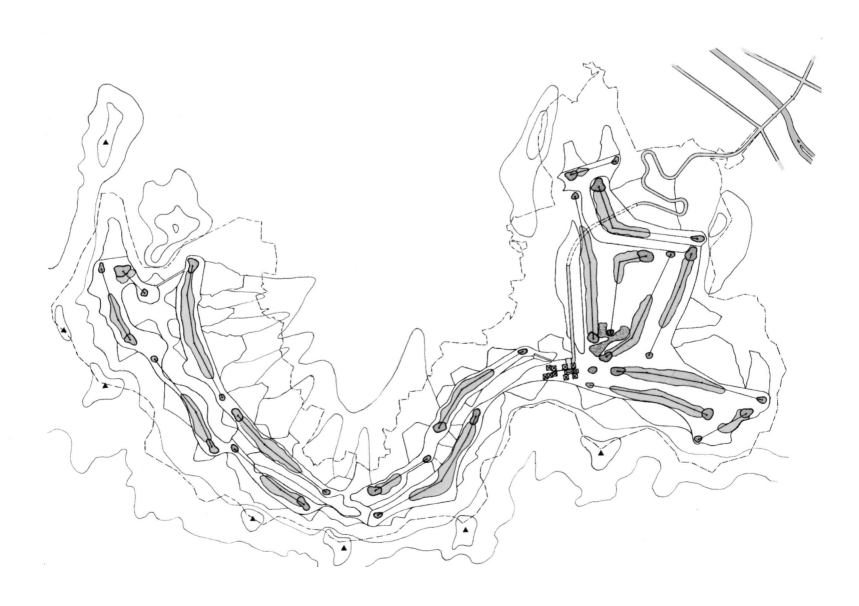

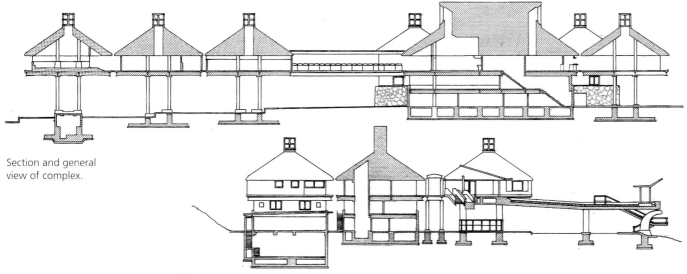

Section and general
view of complex.

An image of the
reception hall and plans
of first floor.

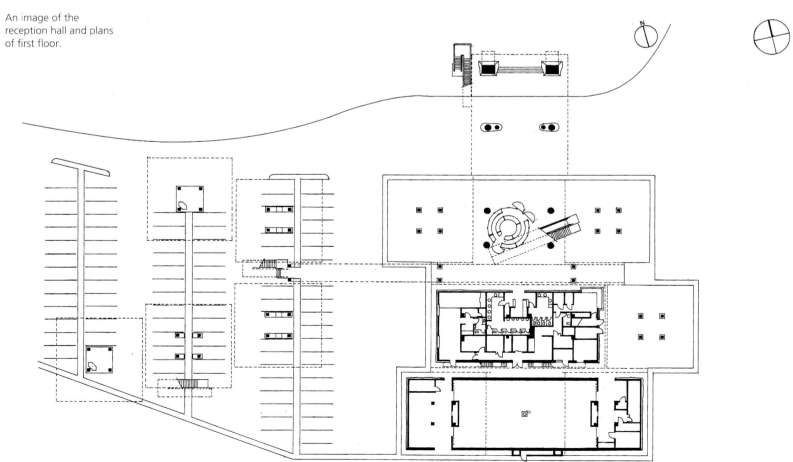

The restaurant and plan
of second floor.

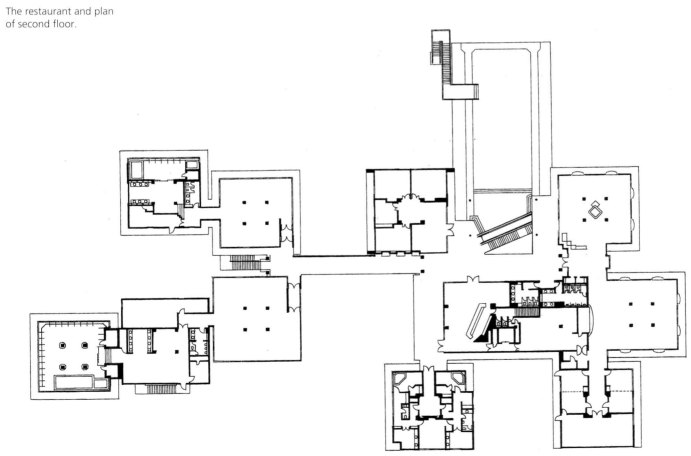

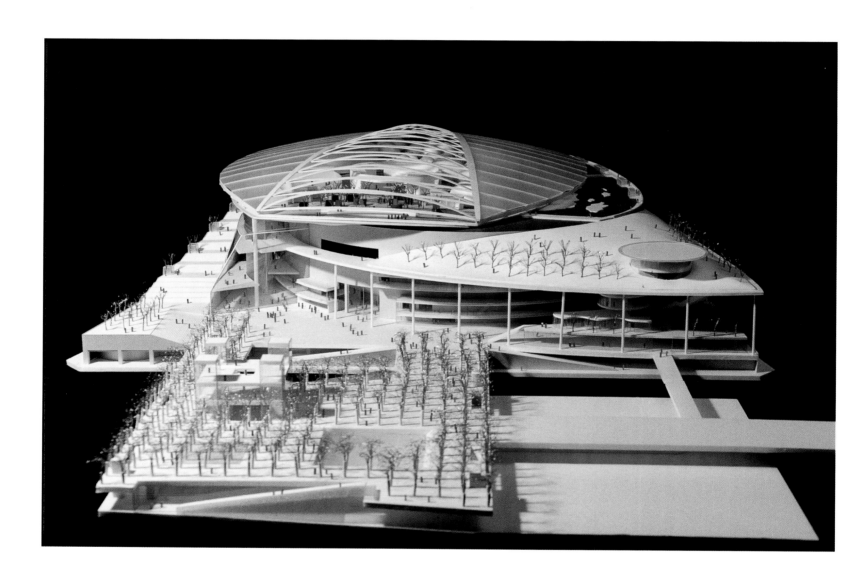

Saitama Arena
1995

The "Saitama Arena" is planned in Saitama, a northern nucleus city of the greater Tokyo Metropolis. This city is growing at the border of the sprawling giant city, by corroding the agricultural villages. The concept of this proposal is to alter the direction of growth of an artificial environment which has been destroying nature, toward the opposite direction of a harmonious relationship with nature.

The "event space" for musical and sport functions and the "cultural amusement space" are sandwiched in between the information transmission space which is called "Interactive Space". The theme of the "cultural amusement space" occupying the upper area is the green. Its concept is the restorationof nature. Recognizing the axis formed between the Hikawa Sando Shrine, located at the proximity of the project site, Saitama Square with its landscape plan, and the project site, the cultural amusement space is named "Forest of the Future" which will be the prototype for harmonious natural and artificial environments. The event space is fitted with much apparatus to vary its spatial size in order to permit various types of events.

The relationship between the city and nature will become prominent with these two spaces when they are filled with a myriad of vibrant performances.

The structural composition of stacking two dichotomous spaces: that of "motion" and of "stillness" on top of each other reflects the contradiction of the modern city.

This project endeavors to comply to the expectations of the public and to fulfill the complicated demands of modern cities that have each of two spaces securing strong independency at times, being complementary or becoming one at other times.

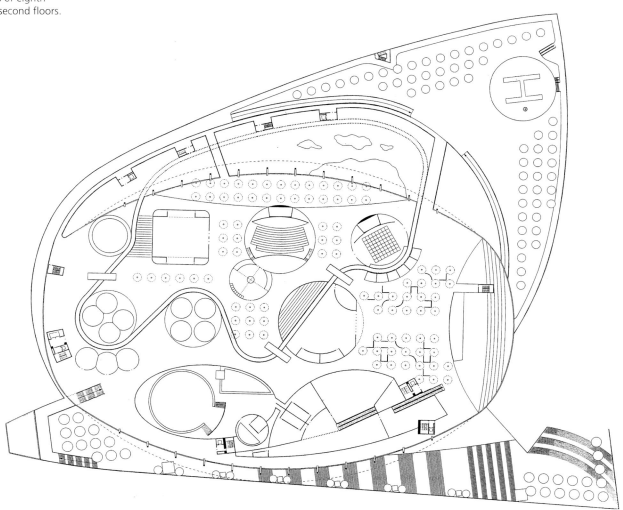

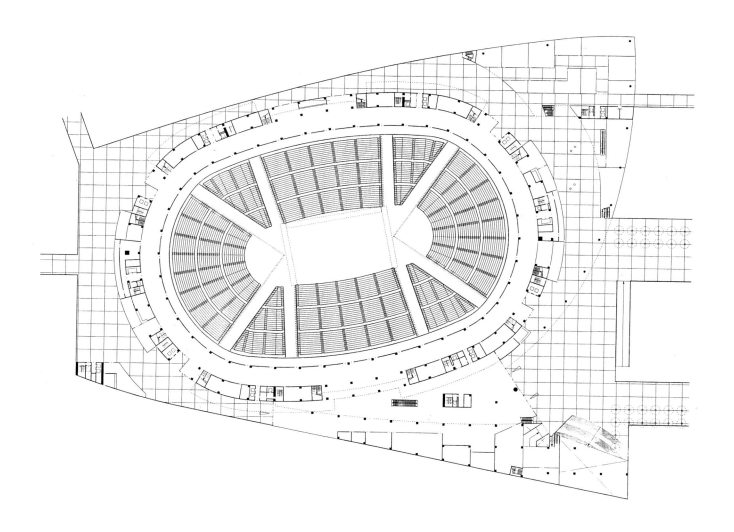

A section of the model
and a detail
of the complex metal
carpentry of the roofing.

Two lateral views
of the model and
two computer images
of the structures.

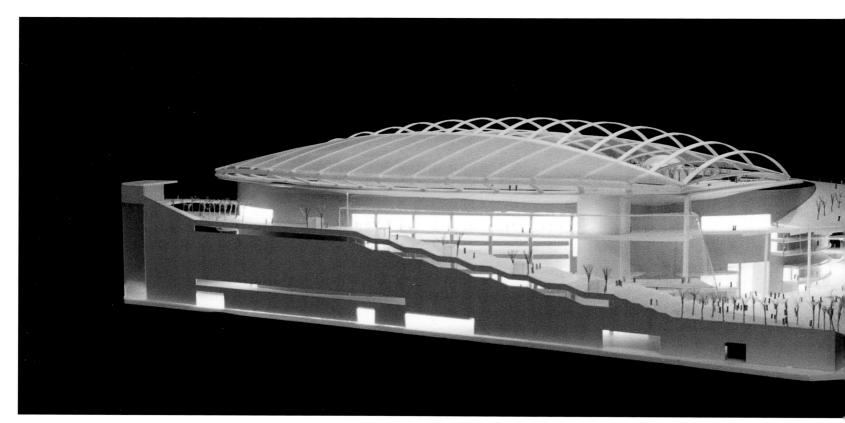

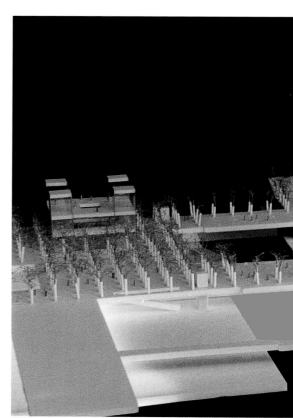

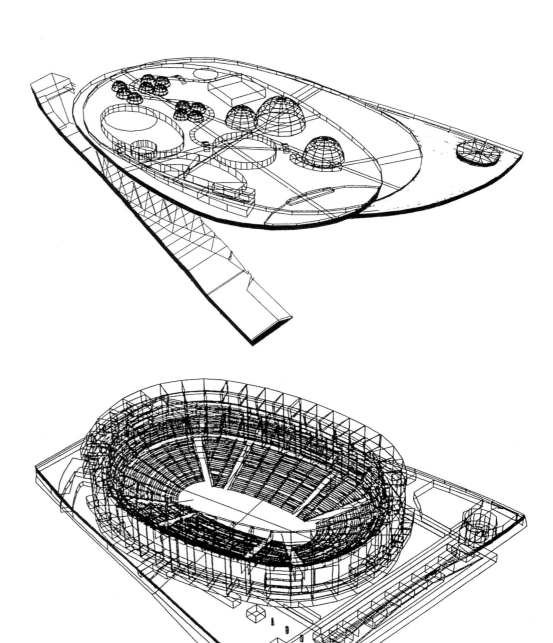

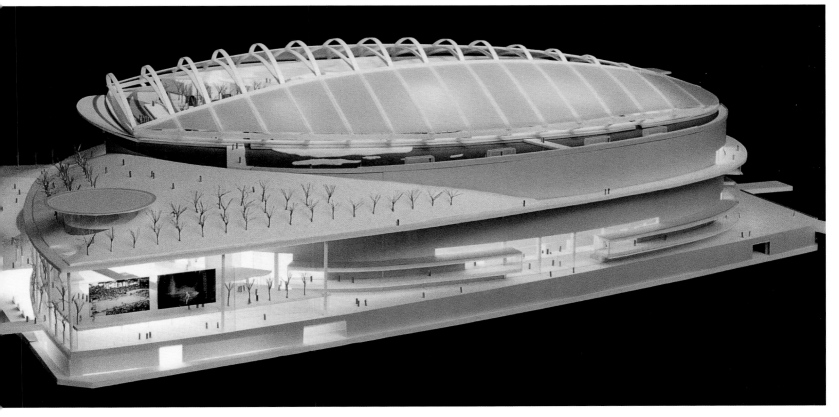

The structures foreseen for the interior of the big metal roofing.

Buildings, facilities and functional spaces around the arena.

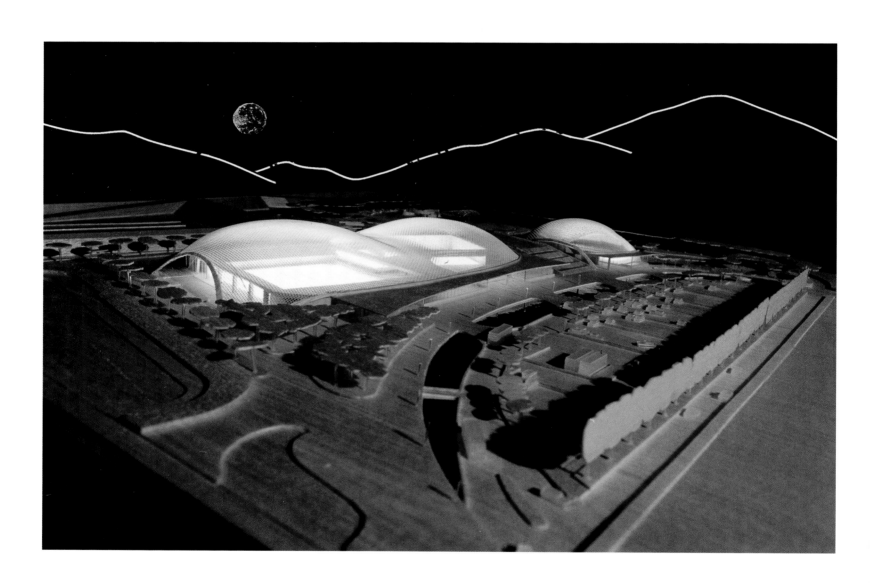

Toyama Prefecture Multi - Purpose Arena 1995

In the proposals for the competition for the Toyama Prefecture arena and for the heated swimming pool of Tonami City, a newly developed shell of wood lattice and membrane is composed as an enticing model.

The shape is one of the distinctions of this building and it is also in harmony with its surrounding scenery. The most outstanding form has been adopted for this building to harmonize with the beautiful natural scenes, as it stands with the mountain range in the background. Another uniqueness is the wooden lattice and the membrane that covers the arena. Having a soft and unique silhouette, at night the dome provides the citizens with a feeling of intimacy, a soft image similar to that of "*chochin*" (Japanese paper lantern). Third, this comfortable environment can be utilized throughout all the seasons in this district where snow falls heavily and the rainy season is long. Fourth, a minimal energy architecture has been realized, which incorporates natural lights, natural draft and ventilation. Fifith, it can effectively utilize the prefecture resources, i.e., the lumber industry.

The uniqueness of the interior construction is the location of the entrance lobby in the center and the arrangement of the training rooms between the large and the medium size arenas. By this arrangement, each of the mutual spaces appears continuous, the space that is utilized most is at the center and the atmosphere of the entire space seems to be always filled with energy.

Since both the arena and the pool are independently covered with a membrane, the shapes are easily distinguished from the outside.

The front of the facility is all for parking. It is divided by ponds for easier utilization, as well as to enhance the exterior view. This proposal shows the direction to proceed for those facilities that hold a close adherence between the citizens and their daily utilization of these functions.

Plans of first
and second floors.

Longitudinal and
tranvsersal sections
and a view of the
model.

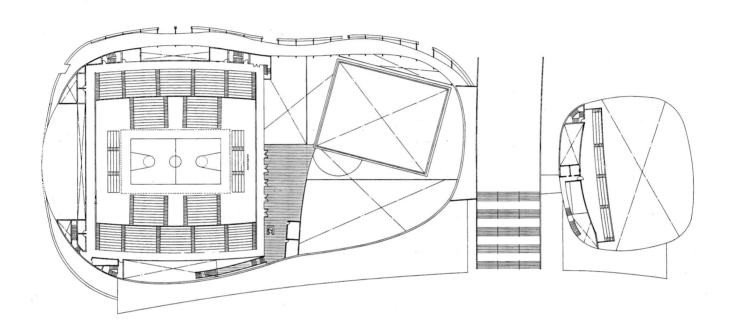

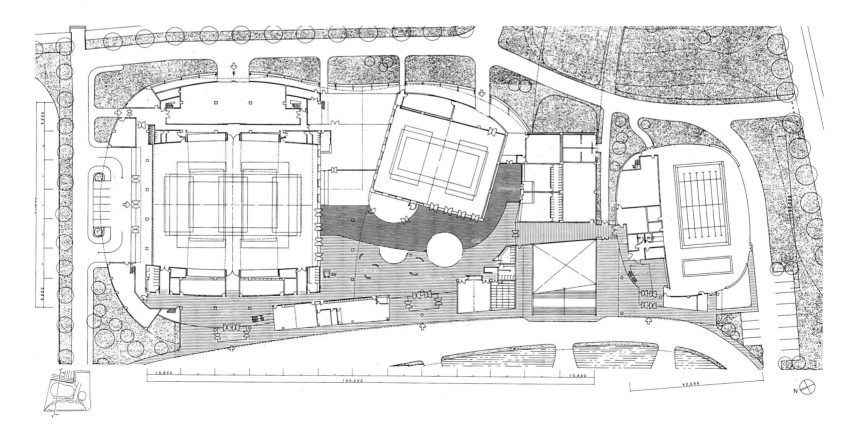

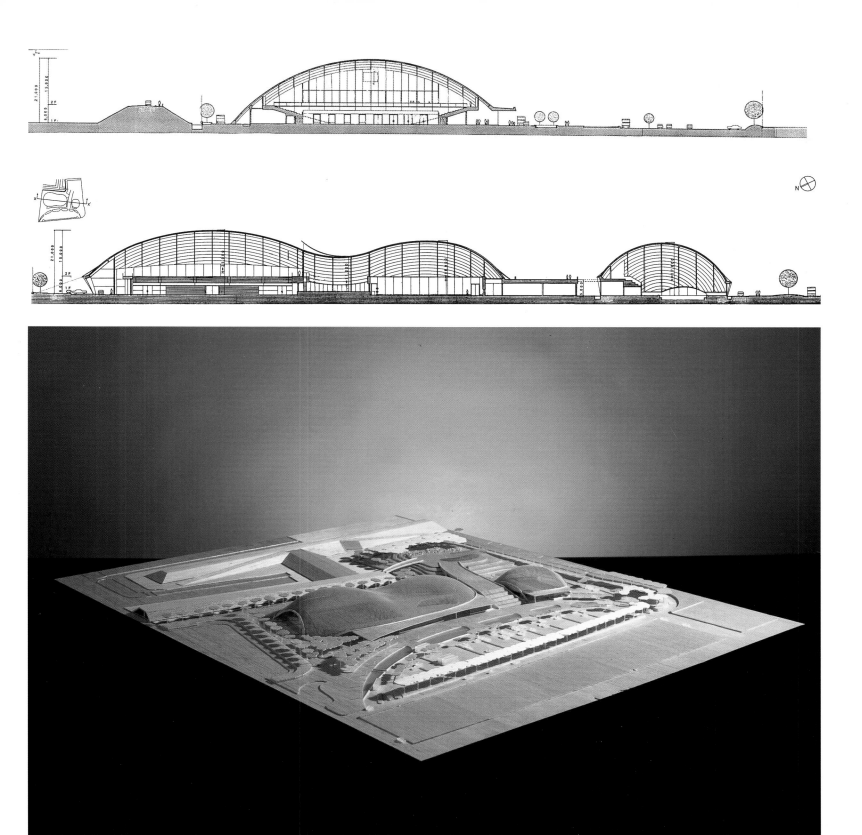

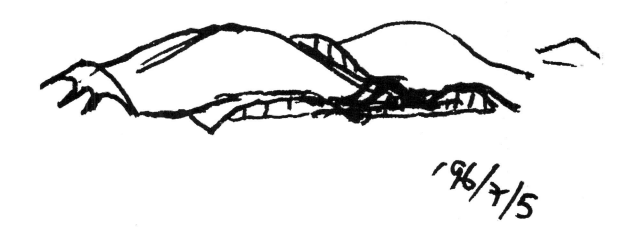

'96/7/5

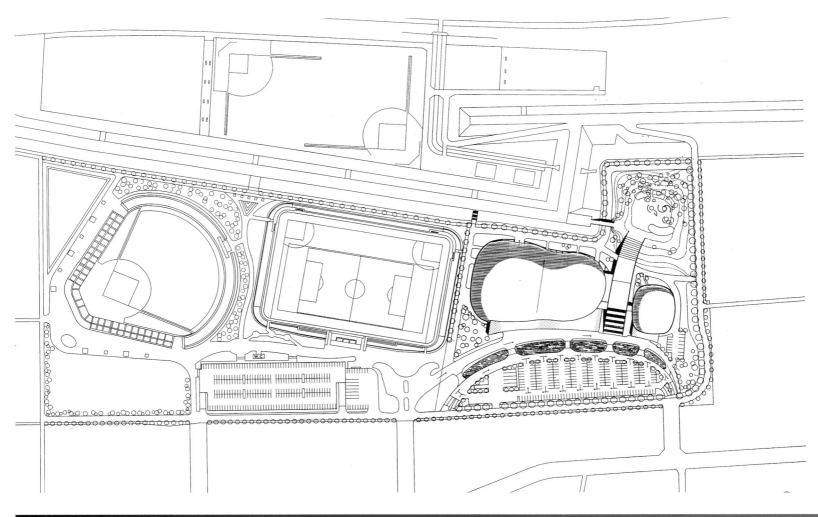

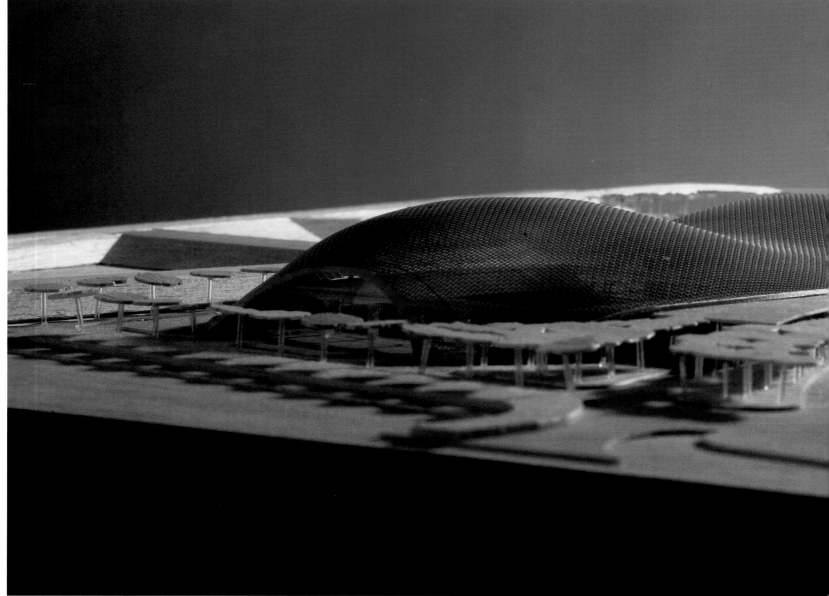

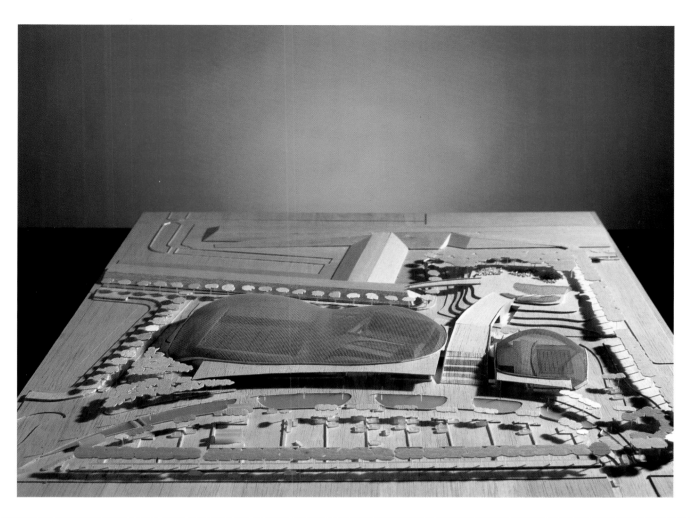

Two views of model
and, next page, general
plan.

Okinawa Museum Complex 1996

This project "blended" an art museum and a natural history museum together. It is a bold thesis presentation to the present-day culture. Today, discipline segmented into arts, natural history, anthropology, etc. can hardly cope with or contribute to the changing world. A new concept on order is to be called "cultural mix". Today's needs call for complex facilities such as these, i.e. the Okinawa Museum.

To this plan, a third construction named "Catalysis Garden" was centrally added. In time, this should begin to function as an Asian information center for the world. In this complex, an art museum and a natural history museum oppose each other and then befriend each other. Functions of each face the other's, and both open up adequately to the "Catalysis Garden."

On the peripheral parts of all the facilities there are a sunlight-controlable loggias, accessible from all directions.

These loggias guide visitors from the approach space to the "Catalysis Garden."

This page and next
page, top, two sections
of complex; bottom,
a view of the model
and general plan.

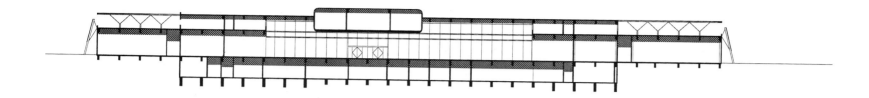

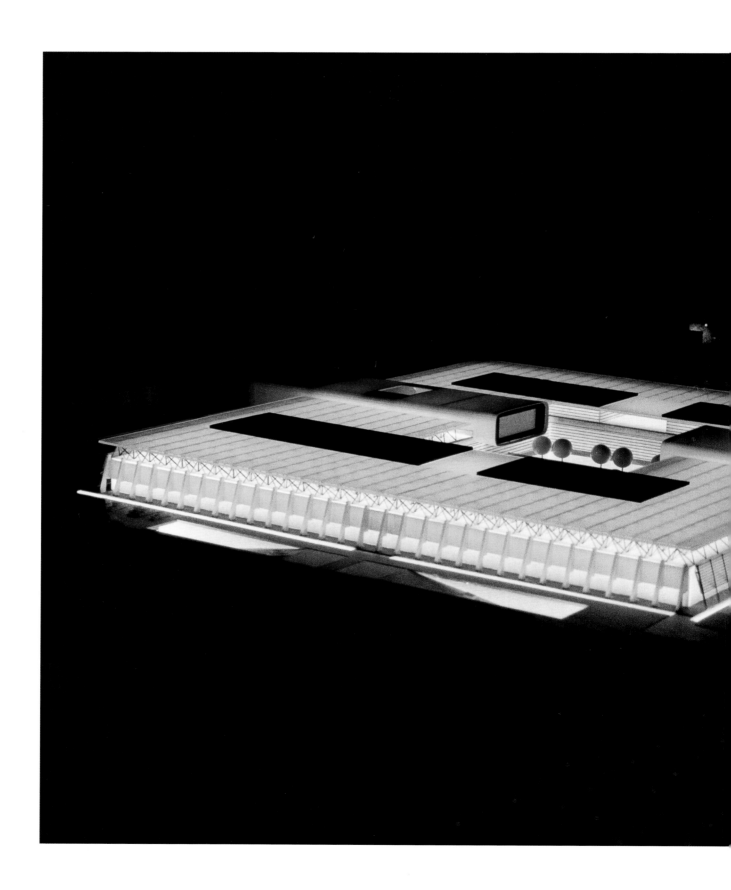

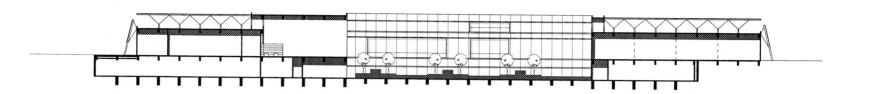

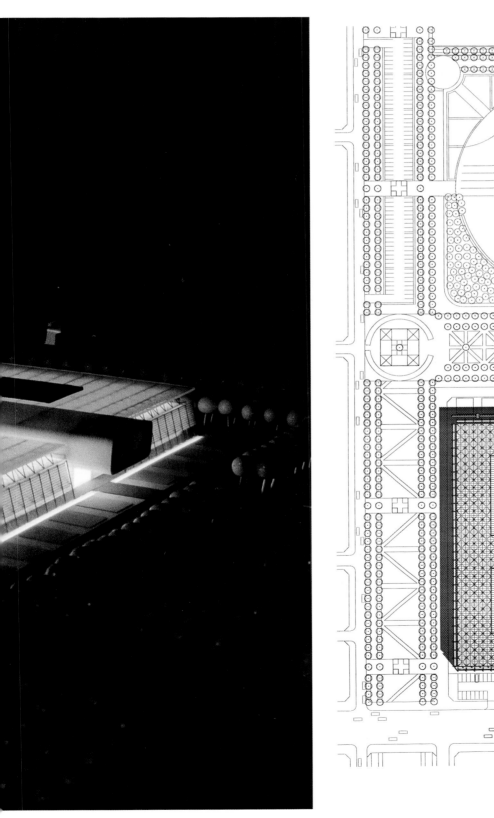

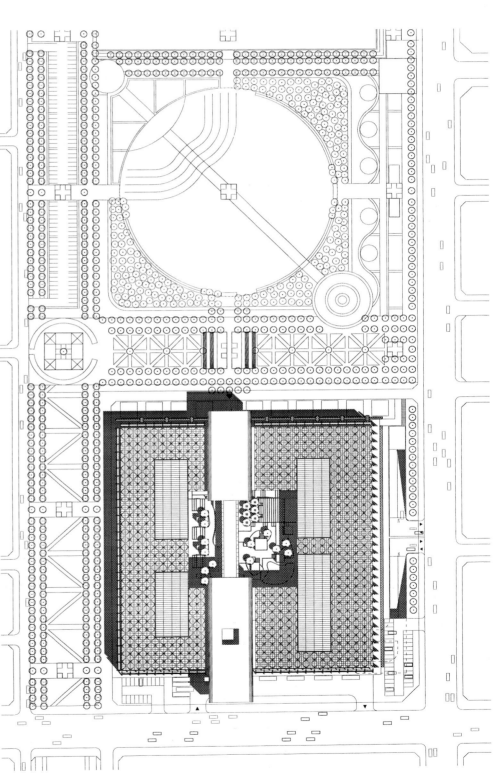

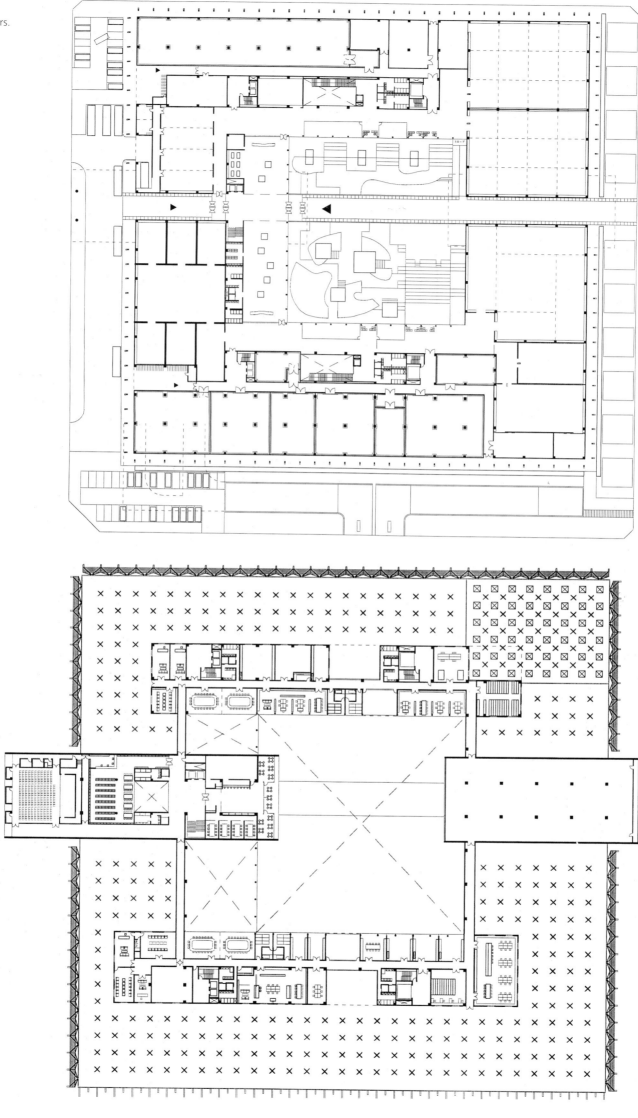

A general view
of the model.

Media-dome of Kita-Kyushu 1998

Our country's largest steel capital, Kita-Kyushu, has environmental problems and beckons the withdrawal of its industries. This multi-purpose dome for Kita-Kyushu has been assigned the role of instigator to initiate the transformation from an industrialized city to a new city of visual information.

This facility will be the outcome of a proposal to start a prize competition which, even in our country is a rare fact since it combines design, construction and management.

Of the many merits of this competition, one is that it allows for a plan that will greatly influence the usage of the facility. Another is that, by keeping its cost within the budget and simultaneously with the events, the image changes of the city from the start to its new objective can therefore be followed. The demerit of the competition is that the architect's expression can easily be that of a common style. One of the rewards is the realization of a low cost and logical compression dome with a minimal rise.

This new dome which was developed with professor Gengo Matsui, has its technology actually applied here for the first time. Its significance is also noticed in the success of achieving a negligible undesirable consequence of sunlight blockage and wind tunnel effects from the surrounding environment due to the shape of this unprecedented dome.

The dome has a length of 200 meters and a width of 150 meters, and it's also one of the largest scale in our country. It can hold 20,000 people for bicycle races and other events, its capacity is of 15,000 people.

Since the dome, which is composed of identical sized framing members and joints, can be assembled and disassembled easily, the construction is simpified and an efficient utilization of natural resources is spurred. Also as a technology which will open the gates to reutilization of materials in the future, the dome possesses qualities which entice many interests.

Furthermore, the design intention for the mechanical system is to utilize as much natural environmental conditions of light, draft and ventilation to attain minimal energy consumption. With its structural and mechanical system, acting as one to hold the cost of operation and administration down, the realization of this tangible dome gives us new hope.

The reason for providing a difference in elevation of one floor between the spectator seats, the bicycle track bank, and the arena, is to create a space that can be used for a variety of events. The uniqueness of allowing the park on the south side to be used together, as one, with this Media Dome will become beneficial in its operation.

Top, the organization
of the arena for sports
events; bottom,
organization for musical
events.

A view of the model
from above, with the
details of the roofing.

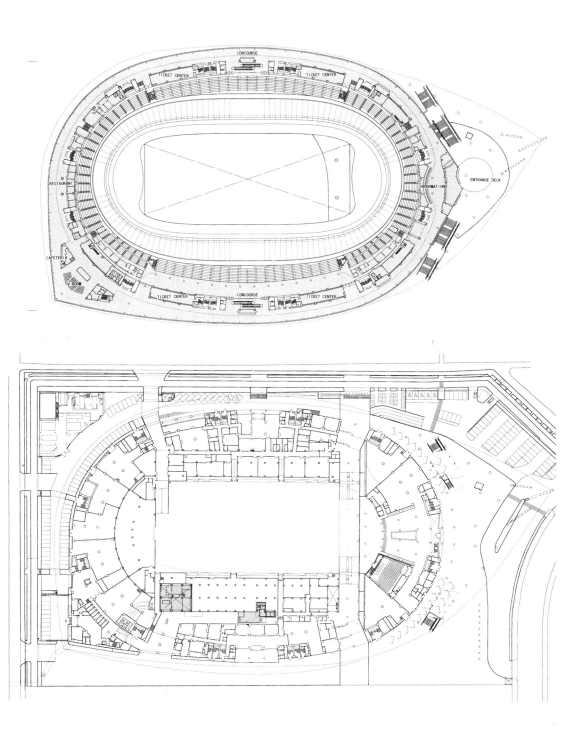

Two views of the model
with images
of the access spaces.

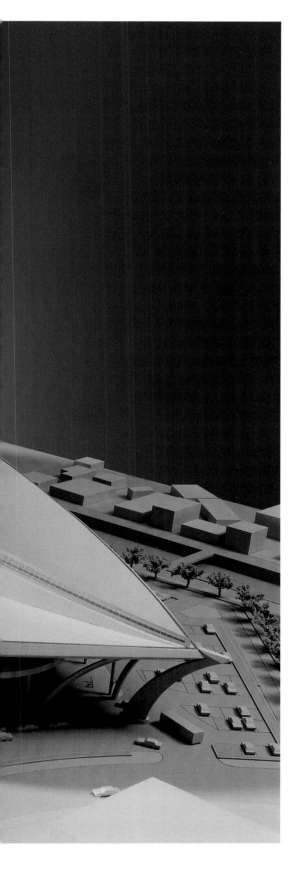

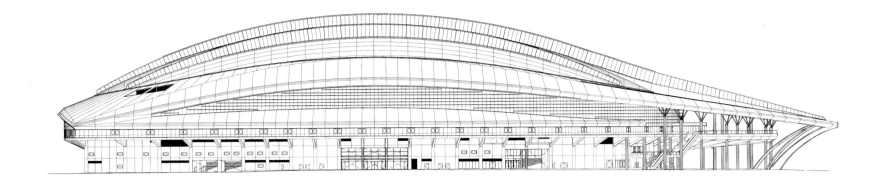

Longitudinal
and transversal sections
of building, detail
of stairs accessing
to upper levels and a
general view of the
building.

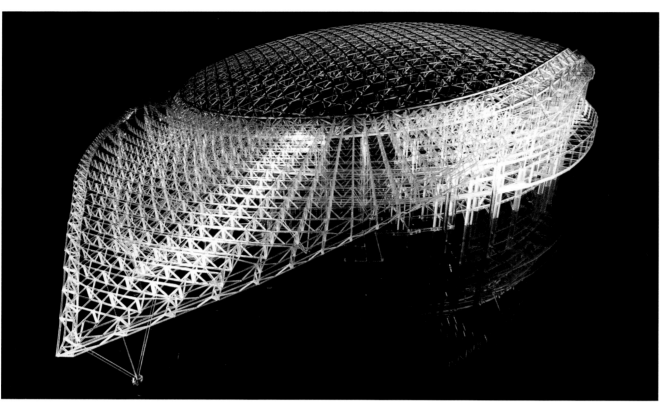

Image of complex roof-beam structure. Below another image of the model.

There view of the
model with various
details of the structure.

Lake - side Art Museum 1999

The museum's chosen site which has a beautiful scenery along the shore of Lake Shinjiko is in a magnificent and blessed environment. For this reason, the main theme for the museum is that it be in harmony with the lake.

Among the many bewitching natural sceneries created by the water side, the sandy beach is selected as theme and the museum is designed as its extension. The roof is held low. Its organic shape with a gentle curve runs along in continuity with the lake as it shelters the space from the northern wind of the lake. It has a soft exterior image, that blends harmoniously and deeply with the environment.

The uniqueness of the museum along the shore of a lake astounds the visitors who, approaching, see through the glass wall and beyond the open lobby, into the beautiful scenery of the sandy beach and the lake.

In the parking lot surrounded by a glass screen, pine trees and rocks are scattered to create a peaceful atmosphere for the appreciation of fine arts.

The image of this rock garden will uplift the feelings of the visitors. The glasses at the front of the yard, the open lobby and the view of the lake, illuminated by rows of lights, will be doubly emphasized when seen at night from the opposite shore of the lake.

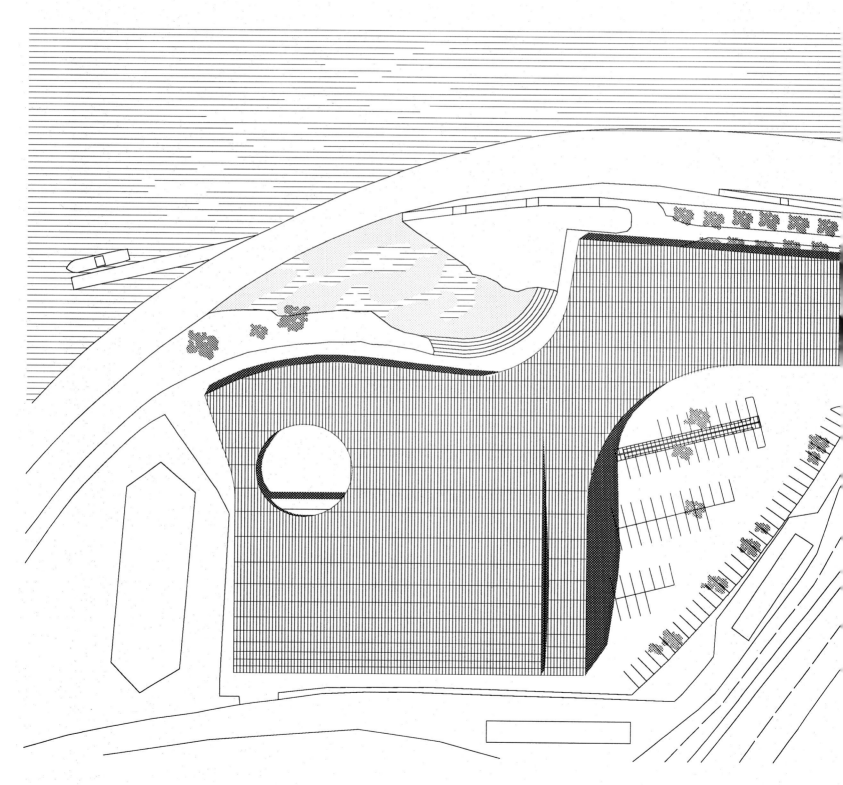

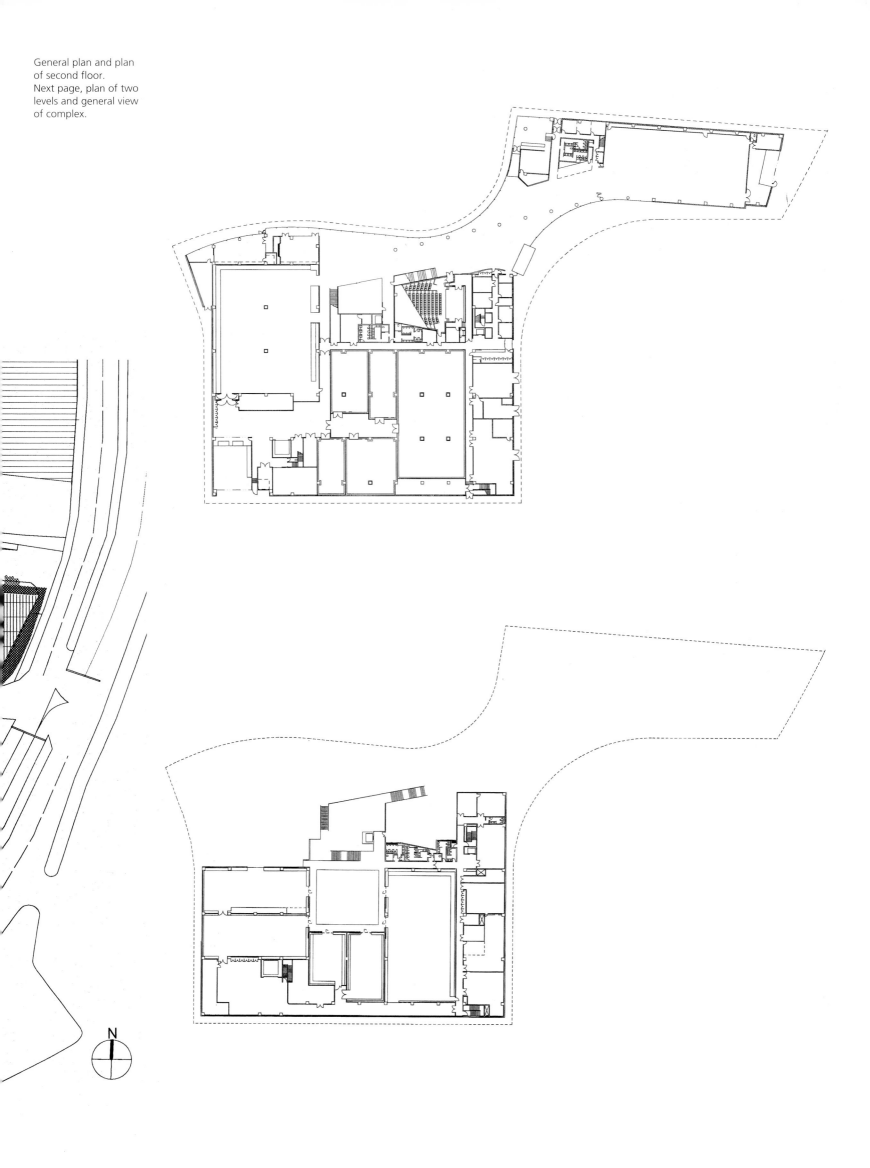

General plan and plan
of second floor.
Next page, plan of two
levels and general view
of complex.

N

From top to bottom,
eastern, southern,
western, and northern
facade.

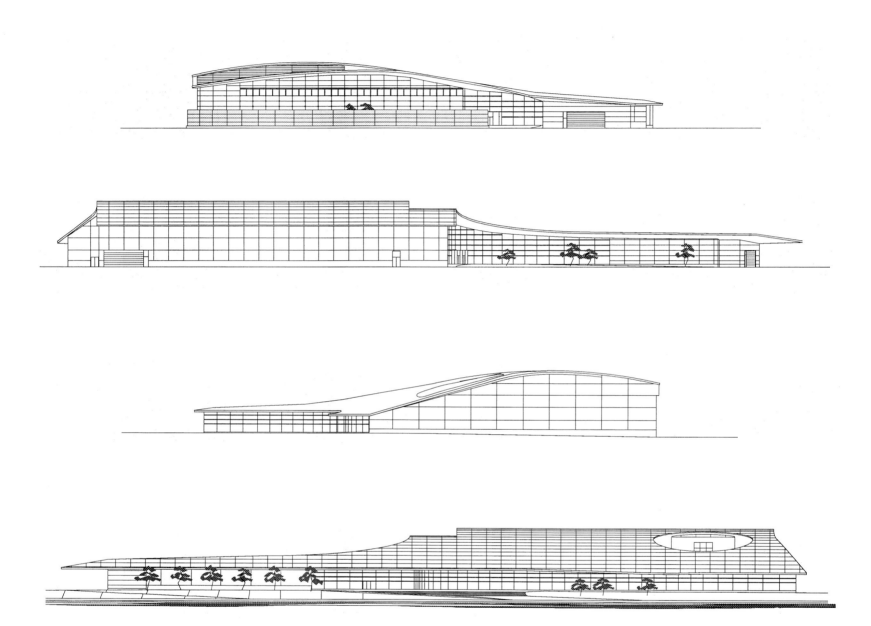

An impressing image
of complex.

A view of the lake side
of building.

Habiter-Marine City

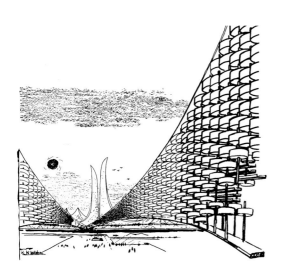

It can not be stated that in the 20th century, man has succeeded in the construction of a genuine artificial environment on land.

The objective of the floating marine city project is to challenge the problems of the artificial environment while coexisting in harmony with the sea, one of the unknown elements of nature.

Experiments have been carried out on the floating marine city using the floating platform tecnologies (an artificial urban base).

A stable and balanced artificial land uses natural resources efficiently by recycling energy, water and other assets as much as possible to create a sustainable environment. The primary objective of the floating marine city is to harmonize with the ocean and to find a way to coexist.

The main reasons for taking into consideration the oceans are population explosion, urbanizations and especially, the absence of renewability of the cities. The existing cities have lost the forces to counter the raging and agitated societies which invite overcrowdedness and chaos.

As the era of new world environment is being welcomed, the important thing is the necessity to examine all the possibilities of whatever types of habitable environment that can be created with the artificial materials whose supply has become abundant in this century. I believe, that is the significance of the "Floating Marine City".

Had it not been for the realization of the concept of the floating marine city, one would not have understood its significance and importance until much later.

The problems of whether a culture can be born or not in the artificial environment will become an issue in the near future.

Had not the artificial environment resulting as a product of industrial revolution become an issue, the accumulation of a new culture would not have appeared as a fresh and vivid theme.

The issues on the artificial environment created with artificial materials will become a new problem which will gradually becom familiar to mankind throughout the 20th century.

From a historical point, this will become the epoc-making theme of the new century.

Marine Communication
City, 1983.

Hawaii Floating City,
1971.

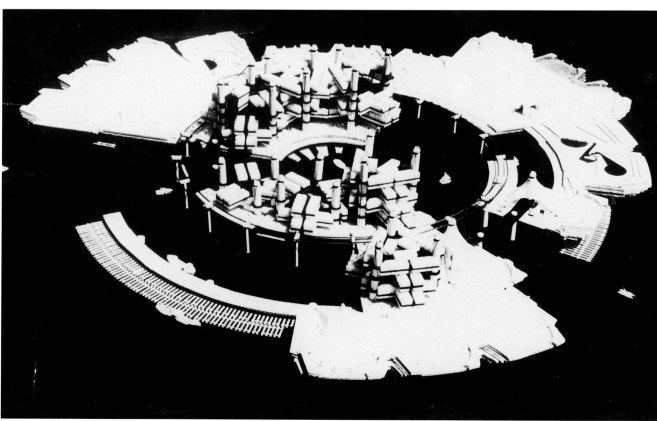

Monaco Floating
Marine City, 1992.

Habiter-Ecopolis

The U.N. has warned that people on earth shall undergo a "*habiter crisis*" toward the end of this century or the beginning of the 21st century. It is expected that by the end of this century, 50% of the world population that lives in urban communities will bring about a vast population increase in the developing countries and people will leave rural communities and flow into the cities. "*Habiter crisis*" is a problem concerning modern cities. Contemporary architecture now faces this crisis throughout the world. As an architect, I would like to present my view for a solution of this problem.

This concept is influenced by the " modernization of tradition process".

Why does the architecture that is designed to improve the environment so often worsen it? In such cases I believe that there must be some inconsistencies within the design methodology employed.

What we must do now is find a way to design a building which harmonizes with the surrounding environment over a long range of time. In search for a new paradigm for the living environment I suggest that Japan should play a significant role. I firmly believe this because Japan has become the best in the world in almost every industrial aspect that is required for living in a contemporary environment. As a result of the industrial revolution, Japan now produces steel, glass and cement, along with automobiles, household appliances, ships, machines and computers.

If Japan should propose its own lifestyle environment, I believe it would apply its known traditions and culture which ensure maximum flexibility of space, and therefore various living environments for people.

The ultimate vision of our living environment would be the realization of multiple choices in many aspects, which I believe would enhance humanity.

When this "multi channel" space is realized, environment will diversify and last. For forty years, I have been considering the vision of a future environment through the projects of "Habiter". My vision is created by a combination of Japanese tradition and the new logic of the artificial environment.

This is what lies beneath my idea of Metabolism and Eco-polis, which address the problems of contemporary cities.

Ecopolis, tree shaped
housing.

Ecopolis, Urban multi-amenity housing.

Stratiform Structure
System.

List of works

1948
HIROSHIMA CATHOLIC CHURCH
OF PEACE (competition)
Hiroshima

1954
INOUE, IJICHI HOUSE
Urawa city, Saitama

1956
ISHIBASHI CULTURE CENTER
Kurume city Fukuoka

TONOGAYA APARTMENT HOUSE
Totsuka-ku, Yokoama

1958
SKY HOUSE
Otsuka Bunkyo-ku, Tokyo

URYU HOUSE
Shibuya-ku Tokyo

1959
NARIMASU KOSEI HOSPITAL
Itabashi-ku, Tokyo

ARI HOUSE
Fukuoka city Fukuoka

SHIMANE PREFECTURAL MUSEUM
Matsue city, Shimane

1960
BS. YOKOHAMA FACTORY GYM
Yokohama city, Kanagawa

HOZUMI HOUSE
Bunkyo-ku Tokyo

TOMIIE WEEKEND HOUSE
Miura-gun Kanagawa

1961
HITOTSUBASHI JUNIOR HIGH
SCHOOL GYM
Chiyoda-ku, Tokyo

1963
SHIMAZAKI HOUSE
Fukuoka city, Fukuoka

"CHO-NO-YA" ADMINISTRATIVE
BUILD.OF IZUMO SHRINE
Hikawa-gun, Shimane

TATEBAYASHI CITY HALL
Tatebayashi city, Gunma

KYOTO INTERNATIONAL
CONFERENCE HALL (competition)
Kyoto city, Kyoto

1964
ASAKAWA APARTMENT HOUSE
Yokohama city, Kanagawa

DINING HALL OF THE TOKYO
ORIMPIC VILLAGE
Shibuya-ku, Tokyo

HOTEL TOKOEN
Yonago city, Tottori

SUZUKI HOUSE
Ohta-ku, Tokyo

1965
TOA RESIN CO., LTD.SAGAMI FACTORY
Zama city, Kanagawa

IWATE EDUCATIONAL HALL
Morioka city, Iwate

TOKUUNJI TEMPLE COLUMBARIUM
Kurume city, Fukuoka

MORIOKA GRAND HOTEL
Morioka city, Iwate

1966
SINKAI HOUSE
Nerima-ku, Tokyo

SURUGA BANK ISEHARA
CORRESPONDENCE CENTER
Isehara-machi, Kanagawa

PACIFIC HOTEL CHIGASAKI
Chigasaki city, Kanagawa

MIYAKONOJO CIVIC CENTER
Miyakonojo city, Miyagi

SHIMOMURA HOUSE
Kamakura-city, Kanagawa

KODOMO-NO-KUNI LODGE
Yokohama city, Kanagawa

1967
SADO GRAND HOTEL
Ryotsu city, Nigata

IWATE PREFECTURAL. LIBRARY
Morioka city, Iwate

GYM OF TACHIBANA-CHO
Tachibana-cho, Fukuoka

HAGI CIVIC CENTER
Hagi city, Yamaguchi

SHIMANE PREFECTURAL LIBRARY
Matsue city, Simane

1969
KURUME CIVIC CENTER
Kurume city, Fukuoka

OSAKA EXPO TOWER
Senrigahama, Osaka

PERU LOW-COST HOUSING
(competition)
Rima, Peru

1970
SERIZAWA LITERARY MUSEUM
Numazu city, Sizuoka

SIMANE PREFECTURAL MARTIAL
ART HALL
Matsue city, Simane

SHIMIZU HOUSE
Bunkyo-ku, Tokyo

1971
KYOTO COMMUNITY BANK,
SHUGAKUIN
Kyoto city, Kyoto

TOTO PAVILION
Chuo-ku, Tokyo

POMPIDOU CENTER (competition)
Paris, France

1972
KYOTO COMMUNITY BANK, ENMACHI
Kyoto city, Kyoto

1973
MUSEUM BERNARD BUFFET
Sunto-gun, Shizuoka

SHIBAMATA TAISHAKUTEN
Katsushika-ku, Tokyo

1974
PASADENA HEIGHTS
Takata-gun, Shizuoka

SHIGARAKI INTERNATIONAL
COUNTRY CLUB
Kouga-gun, Shigaraki

HAGI CITY HALL
Hagi city, Yamaguchi

1975
AQUAPOLIS
Naha city, Okinawa

KUROISHI HOLP CHILDREN'S HOUSE
Kuroishi city, Aomori

1976
OHTSU-LAKESIDE SHOPPING CENTER
Ohtsu city, Siga

TSUKUBA TECHNOPOLIS TOWER
Niihari-gun, Ibaraki

1979
TANABE MUSEUM
Matsue city, Shimane

1980
RABOUL PEACE MONUMENT
Raboul, Papua New Guinea

DARUMAYA-SEIBU
DEPARTMENT STORE
Fukui city, Fukui

1981
SECOND GYM OF GAKUSHUIN JUNIOR
HIGH SCHOOL AND SENIOR HIGH
SCHOOL
Toshima-ku, Tokyo

TREASURY OF IZUMO SHRINE
Hikawa-gun, Shimane

MODERN ART MUSEUM, KARUIZAWA
Kitasaku-gun, Nagano

1982
KUMAMOTO ARTS & CRAFTS CENTER
Kumamoto city, Kumamoto

1983
TETE DEFENSE COMMUNICATION
CENTER (*competition*)
Paris, France

SULAIMAN COURT REDEVELOPMENT
(*competition*)
Kuala Lumpur, Malaysia

MANO TOWN HALL
Sado-gun, Niigata

1985
SAKAIMINATO MARINER HOTEL
Sakaiminato city, Tottori

TSUKUBA EXPO FOREIGN PAVILIONS
Tsukauba-bun, Ibaraki

1986
MAKUHARI MESSE (*competition*)
Chiba city, Chiba

NAGOYA CULTURAL CENTER
(*competition*)
Nagoya city, Aichi

SEIBU "SEED"
Shibuya-ku, Tokyo

GINZA VALAN
Chuo-ku Tokyo

HIROSAKI COMMUNITY CENTER
Hirosaki city, Aomori

1987
ATTU PEACE MONUMENT
Attu island, Alaska

GINZA THEATRE HOTEL
Chuo-ku, Tokyo

ITO HOUSE
Kamagaya city, Chiba

CULTURAL CENTER, TOSHIMA
Toshima-ku, Tokyo

SEIBU "LOFT"
Shibuya-ku, Tokyo

1988
KANSAI INTERNATIONAL AIRPORT
(*competition*)
Osaka bay

NARA EXPO
Nara park

FUKUOKA CITY HALL
Fukuoka city, Fukuoka

KAWASAKI MUSEUM
Kawasaki city, Kanagawa

1989
TOKYO INTERNATIONAL FORUM
(*competition*)
Chiyoda-ku, Tokyo

OSAKA GOVERNMENT OFFICE
COMPLEX (*competition*)
Osaka city, Osaka

1990
FUKUOKA CONFERENCE HALL
(*competition*)
Chuo-ku, Fukuoka

AKASAKA RESIDENTIAL OFFICE
Minato-ku Tokyo

1991
TOMEI EXPRESSWAY SERVICE AREA,
EBINA
Ebina city, Kanagawa

1992
PUBLIC HOUSING, TAKASAKI
Takasaki city, Gunma

LIBRARY BUILD, TOYAMA ANNEX
CAMPUS WASEDA UNIV.
Shinjuku-ku, Toyama

TEAHOUSE JIZAI-TEI

OITA MARINE CULTURE CENTER

1993
KUMAGAYA 2ND CULTURE CENTER
(*competition*)
Kumagaya city, Saitama

GAKUSHUIN UNIV. FACULTY OF THE
LAW & ECONOMICS
Toshima-ku, Tokyo

NIIGATA THEATER COMPLEX

EDO-TOKYO MUSEUM

1994
INDIA PEACE MONUMENT
Manipur, India

INDONESIA PEACE MONUMENT
Biak island

NETWORK RESORT NANSEI CENTER
HOUSE
Tabiai-gun, Mie

KYOTO COMMUNITY BANK, Main office
Kyoto city, Kyoto

KURUME CITY HALL

KUMAMOTO PREFECTURE PUBLIC
SPORTS PLAZA

HOTEL SOFITEL TOKYO
(HOTEL COSIMA)

HANNO KUSUNOKI COUNTRY CLUB

1995
SAITAMA UNIV. OF NURSING
(*competition*)
Koshigaya city, Saitama

TOYAMA PREFECTURE
MULTI-PURPOSE ARENA

1996
OKINAWA MUSEUM COMPLEX

1998
MEDIA-DOME OF KITA-KYUSHU

1999
LAKE-SIDE ART MUSEUM

Kiyonori Kikutake, Architect
H.F.A.I.A. Ph. D.

Kiyonori Kikutake, born in 1928 in Japan, was the first to propose the "Marine City Project" in 1958. Ever since, he has been presenting the "Floating System" projects. In 1960, Kikutake proposed the concept of Metabolic Architecture which integrates tradition into modernity, expressing the idea seen in "Sky House" and "Izumo Shrine." As for the development of Habitat, Kikutake has been pursuing the realization of marine cities, super highrise housings and mega structures by giving environmental considerations for sustainable development.

Professional Associations
Honorary Fellow, American Institute of Architecture (1971 to present)

Academician, Intenational Academy of Architecture

Adviser (Former President), Japan Institute for Macro-Engineering

President of Tokio Society of Architects and Building Engineers

Correspondent Member, French Academy of Architecture

Awards
UIA (Union International des Architects) Auguste Perret Award (1978)

AIA Pan-Pacific Architecture Citation (1964)

Arts encouragement prizes of the Minister of Education, Science, Sports and Culture (1964)

Recent Literary works
Metabolism, 1960

Marine City, 1973

Works and Method, 1978

Edo-Tokyo Museum, 1989

Works by Kiyonori Kikutake 1, 2, 3

Megastructure, 1995

K. Kikutake Architects
1-10-1 Otsuka Bunkyo-ku Tokyo 112 Japan
Tel. 03-5976-6161
Fax 03-5976-6166
http://www. kikutake. co. jp